The Lindisfarne Gospels

The Lindisfarne Gospels

The English Church and Our Multicultural World

Reflections and Liturgical Resources

Ray Simpson

www.kevinmayhew.com

KM PUBLISHING

First published in Great Britain in 2013 by Kevin Mayhew Ltd
Buxhall, Stowmarket, Suffolk IP14 3BW
Tel: +44 (0) 1449 737978 Fax: +44 (0) 1449 737834
E-mail: info@kevinmayhewltd.com

www.kevinmayhew.com

The publishers wish to thank all those who have given their permission to reproduce copyright material in this publication.

Every effort has been made to trace the owners of copyright material and we hope that no copyright has been infringed. Pardon is sought and apology made if the contrary be the case, and a correction will be made in any reprint of this book.

ISBN 978 1 84867 547 6
Catalogue No. 1501371

Front cover and pages 141-144: The four Evangelists and their symbols, from *The Lindisfarne Gospels* by Janet Backhouse. Reproduced by courtesy of the British Library.

Cover design by Rob Mortonson
Edited by Nicki Copeland
Typeset by Richard Weaver

Printed and bound in Great Britain

Contents

Foreword

I write, not as an expert, but as a hungry pilgrim who picks up crumbs left by the experts, finds them life-giving, and shares them with other hungry spiritual seekers.

I thank the Revd Dr Paul Collins, Vicar of Holy Island, for permission to borrow the copy of the *Lindisfarne Gospels* published by the British Museum in 1923, with an introduction by Eric George Millar F. S. A. and signed by Her Majesty Queen Elizabeth II on the occasion of her visit to Holy Island in 1958. On that occasion she was presented with a book of meditations whose illuminated inscription was inspired by the *Lindisfarne Gospels*. Inspiration has never ceased to flow from the *Gospels*.

Ray Simpson
White House
Holy Island of Lindisfarne
www.raysimpson.org

About the author

Ray Simpson is a Celtic new monastic for tomorrow's world, a lecturer, consultant, liturgist, and author of some 30 books. He is the founding guardian of the international Community of Aidan and Hilda and the pioneer of its e-studies programmes. He is an ordained member of the Christian church and lives on the Holy Island of Lindisfarne. His website is www.raysimpson.org

1. The significance of the *Lindisfarne Gospels*

One of the world's greatest works of art in book form.
William Dalrymple[1]

The book that made Britain.
The Sunday Times[2]

It is 2013. Celebrations mark 1300 years of the *Lindisfarne Gospels.* From Durham and Lindisfarne in Britain, to London and throughout the world, awareness dawns of a neglected and glorious birthright – ripe with insights for our multicultural world.

William Dalrymple described in *The New York Review of Books* how the *Lindisfarne Gospels* found their way – along with other great treasures such as Magna Carta and the earliest copies of *Beowulf, The Anglo-Saxon Chronicle* and *Sir Gawain and the Green Knight* – to the new British Library. He writes:

> The *Lindisfarne Gospels* are now recognised as one of the most important manuscripts in the development of medieval art, as well as a crucial document in the history of Western Christianity. For they are not only one of the great glories of monastic book illumination, they also contain the earliest surviving translation of the gospels into the English language.

The British Library's former curator of illuminated manuscripts, Michelle Brown, has gone some way to bringing the book the attention it deserves by writing a superb study of this great masterpiece, entitled *The Lindisfarne Gospels: Society,*

1. Dalrymple, William, 'The Egyptian Connection', *The New York Review of Books,* 23 October 2008.
2. *The Sunday Times,* 11 May 2003.

Spirituality and the Scribe.[3] My references to Michelle Brown refer to this book unless otherwise stated.

Both the *Lindisfarne Gospels* and the *Book of Kells* were the products of a formative period in British and Irish history when three distinct forces were competing to shape the region's art and culture. The first of these forces was the pagan traditions of the Angles and Saxons, Germanic tribesmen from north-west Europe who had arrived in southern Britain mostly after the withdrawal of the Roman legions in the fifth century. They fought their way north, killing, expelling and driving westward the Celtic British farmers who had lived on the land for millennia. These new arrivals from the continent renamed the landscape, towns and many of the rivers in their own tongue so that only a handful of pre-Anglo-Saxon British words – such as mattock, brock, bannock – remain in use in modern English.

By the time of the illumination of the *Lindisfarne Gospels* around AD700, however, this pagan world was under intense pressure from two rival groups of Christian missionaries operating from different directions.

One of these missions came from the Celtic monks of Ireland, who were working their way south and westward from their base at the abbey of Iona off the west coast of Scotland. This had been built in 563 by an Irish prince, Saint Columba, who founded monasteries across what is now Ireland, Scotland, and northern England. Lindisfarne was established by his disciple Saint Aidan in AD635.

By the early fifth century when the Roman legions abandoned Britain, the imperial religion of Christianity had to a large extent disappeared too, clinging on only in a few isolated communities. But amid the great movements of

3. The British Library, 2003.

peoples that swept through Europe as the 'barbarians' took over much of the western half of the empire, burning the monasteries and looting the libraries, the Celtic fringe of Europe became by default an important centre of Christian civilisation. For almost a hundred years, Western Christianity survived partly by holding on in places like the sea-battered rock pinnacles of Skellig Michael on the stormy southwest coast of Ireland.

Here the Celtic monks learned to write Latin, and copied the manuscripts of the classical writers. They relished their new traditions of literacy and generated a renaissance of book illumination and scholarly commentary that embraced Virgil as well as the sermons of Saint Jerome and the *Vitae Patrum* (the lives of the Desert Fathers). Amid this flowering of creativity, they devised new scripts which became the common form of writing throughout the Middle Ages, produced intricate sacred objects, and illuminated gospel books that are among the greatest glories of medieval art. The theological complexity of these books is such that scholars are only now beginning to grasp their true sophistication.

Meanwhile, a second mission, this time from Rome, had arrived at the Kentish royal seat of Canterbury in the south-east of England in AD597 – around the time that the warrior king of Sutton Hoo was being laid to rest in his ship a little further up the East Anglian coast. At one point, the Roman missionaries wanted to turn back – 'they were appalled at the idea of going to a barbarous, fierce and pagan nation,'[4] according to the Venerable Bede (circa 673-735), a monk of the monastery of Jarrow and the author of *The Ecclesiastical History of the English People*, and who is still sometimes

4. Bede, *The Ecclesiastical History of the English People* Book 2, chapter 12 (Penguin, 2003).

dubbed 'the father of English history'. But under the leadership of Saint Augustine of Canterbury, the mission eventually succeeded in converting the royal house of Kent.

The missionaries had been instructed by the Pope to adapt rather than prohibit pagan practices. Pope Gregory the Great wrote:

> We have been giving careful thought to the English, and have come to the conclusion that the temples of the idols among that people should not be destroyed. The temples are to be aspersed with holy water, altars set up in them, and relics deposited there . . . In this way, we hope that the people may abandon their error and, flocking more readily to their accustomed resorts, may come to know and adore the true God.[5]

Like the Irish, these missionaries also brought with them their own quite distinct artistic traditions. Saint Augustine arrived in Kent with 'many books' and 'approached the king carrying . . . the likeness of our Lord and Saviour painted on a board.'[6] One of these books, the *St Augustine Gospels*, is now in the library of Corpus Christi College in Cambridge, and contains realistic Evangelist portraits in the illusionistic classical Mediterranean tradition which had not been seen in Britain since the departure of the Romans. It could not be more different from the restless and intricate decorative art styles then being produced both by the Anglo-Saxons and the monks of Ireland.

> The place where these three distinct streams of art and culture – pagan Anglo-Saxon, Celtic Irish and Roman-Mediterranean – all collided was the kingdom of Northumbria.

---

5. Ibid., chapter 27.
6. Ibid., chapter 29.

> It was here that the fusion, synthesis and interplay of these very different cultural traditions produced an extraordinary renaissance, sometimes called the Golden Age of Northumbria. In scholarship, this was a period of intense intellectual activity which reached a peak in the writing of the Venerable Bede. In art, the twin peaks of achievement were the *Lindisfarne Gospels* and, in sculpture, the great Ruthwell Cross.[7]

Pope Gregory the Great famously said of the Angles who were sold as boy slaves in Rome: 'Not Angles but angels'.[8] In his book *Called to be Angels*, Douglas Dales suggested that the foundations of Anglo-Saxon spirituality hold the key to two challenges facing the modern English Church. The first of these is the recovery and strengthening of its inherent unity. The second challenge is to evangelise England, and to reinforce the foundations of its most vital values and traditions.[9] My own conviction is that this applies more widely to all the countries of Britain, and in fact to the whole English-speaking world and beyond. A fresh look at the *Lindisfarne Gospels*, and a diving into the spirituality that made them possible, can help us meet these two great challenges.

History is about how we shape memory and draw on it to find identity. It is a cumulative heritage for renewal of faith. The *Lindisfarne Gospels* are a visible act of witness, bearing fruit in a burst of celebration. This book suggests ways in which it may also bear fruit in the renaissance of a spirituality today that can capture the minds and imaginations of people of many ethnic backgrounds who at present do not feel at home in the Church.

In his book, *Embracing Change: Spirituality and the Lindisfarne Gospels*, Professor Ewan Clayton of Brighton,

7. *The New York Review of Books*, October 2009.
8. Bede, *The Ecclesiastical History* Book 2 chapter 1.
9. Dales, Douglas, *Called to be Angels* (Canterbury Press, 1998), p.3.

formerly a Benedictine monk at Worth Abbey and now a visiting professor at Sunderland University, observes that several passages are highlighted in light grey. In the light of the glorious illuminations this might go unnoticed and unremarked upon, but he asks why these particular passages should be singled out in this way. He, along with Michelle Brown and other scholars, believes that the *Gospels* were intended to make a statement. Other church centres such as Hexham and Jarrow were consulted. I have heard Professor Clayton argue, in a lecture on Holy Island, that the *Gospels* may be a kind of first manifesto of a truly English Church. Hitherto the northern English churches had been led by the Irish and the southern English churches by the Italians. Here was the first 'leader product' that was English in its origin and in its mission statement. Clayton argues that the three highlighted passages may be taken to represent the typical spirituality of Cuthbert and the emerging English Church.[10]

Three highlighted passages are the Beatitudes, the Parable of the Lost Son and the Temptations of Jesus. Clayton believes these were chosen to illustrate three peaks of Cuthbert's spirituality: his pure gentleness, his mastery of evil spirits and his generous forgiveness and compassion. These are all monastic values. The Beatitudes, or 'Beautiful Attitudes', speak of the simplicity and vulnerability of the original faith and its monastic expression. The Parable of the Lost Son speaks of the compassion and hospitality at the heart of God which is meant also to be at the heart of the Church. The Temptations speak of 'desert spirituality' – the reality of the spiritual struggle at both a natural and a supernatural level. Only in the context of ceaseless devotion can these flowers of

10. Clayton, Ewan & Cooper, Robert, *Embracing Change: Spirituality and the Lindisfarne Gospels* (Clare Clayton, 2003), p.35.

beautiful attitudes, ceaseless prayer and hospitality flourish. Clayton also notes that the Carpet is in the shape of a cross, a reflection of Cuthbert's mission journeys when they set up a preaching cross.

The suggestion that these highlighted passages may offer a clue as to the original priorities of the English Church may also shed light on the Church's contemporary predicament. The top-down Christendom model of Church with its dioceses, bishops' thrones and parishes served us well for part of the second millennium but is now withering away. In response to this crisis we are seeing the rise of fresh expressions of church and of new monasticism. Some who labour faithfully in the inherited Church fear, however, that these are peripheral distractions. The message of the *Lindisfarne Gospels* is that a monastic way of life is fundamental to the whole Church in England.

Bede tells us that Aidan introduced a Rule to English-speaking people, not just to the monks. New monasticism is seeking that 'something' that has been edged out of many churches.

The late Ian Harland, who was Bishop of Carlisle and Soul Friend to the Community of Aidan and Hilda, once said to me, 'I think we are coming to the end of the parish phase of church.' He added, referring to monastic churches in Ireland and Britain, 'It has happened before.' In my book *High Street Monasteries: fresh expressions of committed Christianity*, I explore ways in which monastic experiments can become churches and ways in which traditional churches may become monastic.[11] But beyond all the changes in practices and forms, we need a change in the values of the

11. Kevin Mayhew, 2009.

Church, and fresh ways of connecting with the unchurched from different ethnic backgrounds.

There are plenty of books about the *Lindisfarne Gospels* by academic experts. This book seeks to inspire the contemporary church with user-friendly reflections and resources.

2. The story of the *Lindisfarne Gospels*

In the fifth and sixth centuries, following evangelisation by Saint Patrick and others, pagan Ireland 'began to be described as a land of saints and scholars'.[12] This extraordinary transformation was due to a range of new wellsprings brought by the gospel, combined with ancient wellsprings such as bards and foster mothers who were transformed by the gospel. Most of all, it was brought about by a widespread emergence of churches that were seven-days-a-week spiritual hubs of a tribe or locality, engined by full-time monks or nuns. Many of these developed schools and scriptoriums where the Gospels and psalms could be copied, and in some places beautifully decorated. Saint Columba (died 597) is said to have established more than 300 monastic churches. They were mostly small, although a few, such as Derry and Durrow, were major centres of devotion and learning.

Saint Columba in Ireland and Britain

Columba was passionate both as an evangelist and as a scribe. He therefore spared no pains to obtain or make copies of psalters, Gospels and other valuable manuscripts for his monks. His former tutor at Moville, Finnian, had brought back from Rome the first copy of Saint Jerome's Psalter to reach Ireland. Finnian guarded this precious volume jealously, but Columba surreptitiously made a copy for his own use. Finnian, on being told of this, laid claim to the copy, and won his claim in a court judgement.

---

12. Source unknown.

For whatever reason (some think it was an act of penance associated with the court case and a battle between the tribes of Finnian and Columba that took place some time after in which many were slain), Columba emigrated in around AD563 to the Irish Scots colony of Dalriada in what is now Argyll, Scotland, and established his mother monastery on the island of Iona. From Iona he trekked up the Great Glen beside Loch Ness to meet Brude, King of the Picts, and began the evangelisation of these Brythonic-speaking pagans who lived north of the Irish Scots. On Iona he established a school of Irish calligraphy and illumination based on the system laid down by the mother country (Ireland), which enabled both evangelisation and theological learning sustained by Iona's library.[13]

Conversion of Anglo-Saxon exiles in Britain

During this period, something quite different was taking place further south in Britain. The pagan Anglo-Saxons had colonised much of eastern Britain, pushing many of the original Christian Celtic Britons to the west. The Anglo-Saxons' largest kingdom was Northumbria, which stretched from the river Humber to the Firth of Forth, and from coast to coast. Its royal headquarters were at Bamburgh. When its King Ethelfrith was slain in 616, his sons, who had the legal right to succeed him, fled for sanctuary to the Irish Scots colony of Dalriada on Northumbria's northern border, whose Christian leaders could be trusted. In fact their ruler, whose predecessor had given Iona to Columba for his monastery, formed a treaty with Northumbria's young royal exiles. He fostered them as an extended family and in return,

13. See *Early Irish Minuscule Script* pp.1-4, plate 11.

as the boys became men, they served as warriors for the Dalriadian king. While they were in Iona, monks befriended, taught and baptised them as Christians.

One of Ethelfrith's sons was Oswald. In due course (633) Oswald, who became a devout servant of Christ, steeped in Columba's monastic Irish tradition, regained Northumbria's throne for his family, with the help of his Irish Scots allies, and invited Iona to send monks to evangelise his people.

Saint Aidan's mission to the English

After a failed first mission, the Irish monk Aidan arrived from Iona in 635 with 12 brothers. Aidan's method was twofold. First, the mission brothers were to walk among the people. As they walked they were to memorise, meditate on and share the gospel story. If they met someone, they were first to make friends with them and listen to their concerns and beliefs. Only then were they to ask if their new friend would like to hear what they believed.

Second, they were to model the kingdom of God and create colonies of heaven on earth. So Aidan established a monastery, a school for Anglo-Saxon boys and a scriptorium on the tidal island of Lindisfarne, a few miles from Bamburgh. It was extremely simple, and the buildings were made of wood. If rich people gave Aidan money, he gave it to the poor, or went to the slave market and bought freedom for a slave, perhaps offering them a job at the monastery or even a place at the school. From the start, Aidan aimed to create an indigenous Anglo-Saxon – that is English – Church by training up English leaders. Over the following years many daughter monasteries sprang up near and far.

The leader of the failed mission had tried to impose Irish customs upon the English. Aidan thought that was the wrong way. He taught his brothers to impart the milk of God's word and to allow it to bear fruit in whatever ways were natural to the English.

Aidan's method of spreading the gospel was in stark contrast to those who thought the best way was to make the Church – through its buildings, legal requirements, clergy dress and artefacts – the most impressive and dominant institution in the world. In 735 Boniface, the English missionary to the Germans, commissioned from the abbess Eadburgha a copy of the epistles of Peter written in gold so that, as he said, he might impress honour and reverence for the Scripture before the eyes of the carnal in his preaching.[14] Unlike Boniface, Aidan eschewed outward show: the brothers wore simple garments made of wool, and Aidan refused to ride a horse – only higher classes rode horses. He and his mission brothers walked everywhere.

King Oswald's alliances with four races

Oswald (605–642) proved to be a brilliant king, statesman and sponsor of Christian mission. He not only won battles but he also built alliances with kingdoms of Picts, Celtic Britons and Scots Irish as well as of Anglo-Saxons, who in a few kingdoms had renounced paganism and begun to follow the traditions of the missionaries who had come from Rome to Kent in 597. Oswald's successor, Oswy, extended these alliances. The Pictish kingdom of the Christian King Nectan extended to the northern shore of the Firth of Forth. The Church of Scotland parish of Abernethy claims that the village was once the centre of his kingdom, and that its church was founded by Irish Christians and dedicated to Saint Brigid in the sixth century. The Cymric speaking

14. *Monumenta Germaniae Historia, Epistolae* 111 (1892) p.60.

Britons were spread far more widely than present-day Wales. They populated what is today named Cumbria, after the Cymri. The small Celtic kingdom of Elmet, which covered the area that later became the West Riding, was only conquered by Northumbria in 616 or 626, and would have retained some of its Celtic population.

It is possible that Oswald renewed earlier influences from a brief Roman mission in the royal centre and church at York. He befriended the king of the West Saxons and was godfather at his baptism. Aidan, who had missionary oversight of all the peoples in the large region of Northumbria, was therefore bishop of four races who spoke different languages and who had previously been hostile towards one another. Anglo-Saxons (who became known as the English), Celtic (Welsh-speaking) Britons, and on the northern fringes Picts and Irish Scots now embraced the fellowship of the Christian gospel.

The Church spans political and religious divisions

After Oswald was slain in battle in 642, Northumbria divided into two sub-kingdoms. By popular demand, Oswin ruled the southern kingdom of Deira (mostly today's Yorkshire). Oswy, Oswald's younger brother, ruled the larger northern kingdom of Bernicia from Bamburgh. Both kings wanted Aidan to remain as bishop of all Northumbrians. He was a sign of unity inspired by love, and he spent time in York as well as on Lindisfarne.

Aidan conducted the marriage of Oswy to a queen from Kent who followed the Roman tradition – Queen Eanfled. She sponsored a nobleman who became a monk at Lindisfarne and his attendant, an outstanding young man named Wilfrid who studied at Lindisfarne a year or two before Aidan died in 651. Then the queen sponsored Wilfrid on a visit to Rome; he became a bishop and ever after promoted the glories and pomp of Rome in Northumbria and later in Sussex. The queen's sponsorship of Wilfrid perhaps marked the beginning of the end of the classless society at the monastic school, where sons of noblemen had shared equally with slaves whose freedom Aidan had purchased.

The Synod of Whitby changes the Irish–Roman balance

In 664, Oswy convened a synod of the Northumbrian Church at the Whitby monastery that was presided over by Hilda, the abbess, who was converted through a Roman missionary but who was trained in, and delighted in, the Irish tradition of Aidan. The Irish Bishop Colman of Lindisfarne, and Bishop Wilfrid, who preferred all things Roman to what he regarded as the 'rustic' ways of Lindisfarne, were the chief spokesmen for the two sides in the debate, which some scholars surmise was stage-managed. The Synod decided in favour of Rome on controversial points such as the date of Easter and the tonsure of monks.

Reading between the lines, this Synod affected a host of other things too – it marked a new framework and a new tone. All the Irish monks and 30 English monks left Lindisfarne for Ireland, under Bishop Colman. Two dioceses in addition to Lindisfarne were created at York and Hexham. However, former Irish students at Lindisfarne who had become leaders elsewhere at the time of the Synod of Whitby continued their ministry in Northumbria. English students who had trained in the Irish tradition at Lindisfarne and who had become missionary bishops, such as Chad in York and Mercia (the English Midlands) and Cedd among the East Saxons further south (today's Essex), also continued to exercise their ministries. The *Lichfield Gospels* are named after Chad. We learn from Bede and from a Lindisfarne monk's *Life of Saint Cuthbert* that the English brothers who remained at Lindisfarne disliked the new ways: we may presume that they were the means of handing on the best Irish art which reached its culmination in the pages of the *Lindisfarne Gospels*.

Saint Cuthbert at Lindisfarne

At the request of Lindisfarne's departing Irish Bishop Colman, Eata, who was abbot of the monastery at Melrose and had been one of the first 12 English boys to be trained under Aidan, also became abbot of Lindisfarne. Eata continued to reside at Melrose and put the Anglo-Saxon monk Cuthbert in day-to-day charge at Lindisfarne. The boy Cuthbert had been reared as a Christian under Aidan's mission and had offered himself for monastic service under the direction of Boisil, the Irish prior of Melrose, following Cuthbert's vision of Aidan being escorted into heaven above Bamburgh while Cuthbert kept watch over sheep by night on the Lammermuir Hills. Eata appointed Cuthbert to Lindisfarne 'that he might impart to the brothers with a prior's authority the maintenance of a regular discipline and set an example of the same by his own actions'.[15] Cuthbert gradually mellowed the complaining brothers by his persistent cheerfulness, kindness and prayer, strengthened by prayer vigils at night at a place on the outskirts of the monastery which tradition locates as the islet now known as St Cuthbert's Isle.

The story of Cuthbert, to whom the *Lindisfarne Gospels* are dedicated, is well known. As a Christian boy on the shore by the mouth of the river Tyne, surrounded by a crowd of

15. Bede, *The Life and Miracles of Saint Cuthbert*, chapter 16 quoted in J. F. Webb (trans), *The Age of Bede* (Penguin, 1998).

pagans who mocked monks carrying wood to build a new monastery on their wind-blown boats, he gained their respect by praying and causing the contrary wind to cease. As an outstanding student at Melrose, mentored by Boisil, he recovered from plague, preached and healed in remote villages, and mentored young people. As guest master at Ripon, he learned the arts of warm hospitality, and Bede wondered whether he had entertained an angel. Hospitality is enshrined in biblical faith, but in the Irish tradition it shines most brightly.

Bede links the simple common life in the Irish tradition which was shared at Lindisfarne by the entire Church with the teaching of Pope Gregory of Rome, who was himself a monastic:

> Whilst the monastery is governed by the abbot, whom they, with the consent of the brethren, have elected, all the priests, deacons, singers, readers, and other ecclesiastical officers of different ranks, observe the monastic rule in every respect, as well as the bishop himself. The blessed pope Gregory showed that he approved this mode of life, when in answer to Augustine, his first missionary to Britain, who asked him how bishops ought to converse with their clerks, among other remarks he replied, 'Because, my brother, having been educated in the monastic rule, you ought not to keep aloof from your clerks: in the English Church, which, thanks be to God, has lately been converted to the faith, you should institute the same system, which has existed from the first beginning of our Church among our ancestors, none of whom said that the things which he possessed were his own, but they had all things common.' When Cuthbert, therefore, came to the church or monastery of Lindisfarne, he taught the brethren monastic rules both by his life and doctrines, and often going round, as was his custom, among the

> neighbouring people, he kindled them up to seek after and work out a heavenly reward. Moreover, by his miracles he became more and more celebrated, and by the earnestness of his prayers restored to their former health many that were afflicted with various infirmities and sufferings; some that were vexed with unclean spirits, he not only cured whilst present by touching them, praying over them, or even by commanding or exorcising the devils to go out of them; but even when absent he restored them by his prayers, or by foretelling that they should be restored.[16]

After his time as prior of Lindisfarne, when he was loyal to the Roman framework, Cuthbert obtained permission to be a hermit prayer warrior on the rugged Inner Farne Isle. Bede says, 'At the entry of our soldier of Christ . . . the devil fled and his host of allies with him.'[17] Finally, in obedience to an earlier prophecy, he bowed to pressure to become a bishop and was consecrated Bishop of Lindisfarne in 685. Tradition says that his labours as bishop took him as far north as St Andrews, whose university is said to have started with a Christian community he planted there. Kirkcudbrightshire is named after him. He laboured as far west as Carlisle. By then separate dioceses had been created in more southerly parts of Northumbria such as Hexham and York.

Contacts with Rome increased after the Synod of Whitby, and there was a danger of polarisation between the Irish and Roman traditions in the English Church. The aged Cuthbert returned to Farne Isle to die, though he acknowledged reluctantly that the brothers would take his body to Lindisfarne

16. Bede, *Life and Miracles of St Cuthbert*, in a volume entitled *Ecclesiastical History of the English Nation*, trans. J. A. Giles, Everyman's Library 479, (London: J. M. Dent; New York: E. P. Dutton, 1910), p.286-349.
17. Bede, *Life and Miracles of St Cuthbert* quoted in Webb, J. F. (trans) *The Age of Bede* (Penguin Classics, 1998).

for burial. He did not wish his tomb to become a focus for schismatic tendencies. His dying words to his brothers, recorded by Bede, therefore form a significant part of the Lindisfarne tradition:

> I would much rather you left the island, taking my bones with you, than that you should be a party to wickedness on any pretext whatsoever, bending your necks to the yoke of schism.[18]

Cuthbert was a champion of unity in diversity. He worked loyally under the new framework, but he continued Celtic British and Irish practices such as praying while standing in water, repairing to deserted places, meeting with a soul friend and rejoicing in creation.

He had the pragmatism which characterises the English to the present day. He also had the virility of the Anglo-Saxon, tempered by the deep, tender kindness of Christ.

Trade routes and the Lindisfarne Scriptorium

Pilgrimage routes to the continent were opened again after having been considered too dangerous for a century. Trade ships from further afield brought their products to Northumbrian ports. No description of the scriptorium at Lindisfarne exists, but we can piece together quite a lot of information about typical Northumbria scriptoria at that time and shortly after.

It has been reckoned that at least 130 calves gave their skins for the parchment of the *Lindisfarne Gospels* alone. Each sheet of calf skin formed two leaves (four pages) of the book. The sheets were soaked, scraped and stretched. Four

18. Ibid., p.95.

large sheets were placed together and folded, making sixteen pages. Bishop Eadfrith inscribed these before they were bound together. With the help of a ruler, tiny holes were pricked down each side of the pages to serve the same purpose as do lines today. Eadfrith used either quill or reed pens. Ink was made from oak-galls and iron salts to an extremely good recipe. The 45 colours used for the illustrations were made from an astonishing range of ingredients derived from animal, vegetable and mineral sources: The artist must have been a skilled chemist. He developed an extensive colour palette including:

- Purples, crimsons and blues from plant extracts such as woad, lichens and folium (turnsole)
- Yellow from orpiment (trisulphide of arsenic)
- Red/orange from toasted lead
- Green from verdigris, made by suspending copper over vinegar, or by a blue-yellow mix (vergaut)
- White from chalk, crushed seashell or eggshell
- Black from carbon.

Pigments were ground to a fine powder and mixed with adhesive beaten egg. Some fine details were added in gold leaf and powdered gold ink. It used to be thought that the ultramarine blue came from lapis lazuli, a precious stone found in the Himalayas. This is now doubted, although some materials were undoubtedly imported from the Mediterranean.

Northumbrian links with Rome

Northumbrian churches forged greater links with Rome. Benedict Biscop, the founder of the two great monasteries at Wear and Jarrow, made three trips to Rome and brought back all kinds of books useful for divine learning. After appointing Ceolfrid as the abbot of Jarrow's monastery of Saint Paul in 681, he made a fifth and final trip to Rome, bringing back many more books and works of art. Benedict planned to take a compendium of books copied at Wear-Jarrow as a gift to Pope Gregory but was prevented by death from personally delivering it. This is identified as a huge volume in the Laurentian Library at Florence and has a bearing on textual and artistic styles in the *Lindisfarne Gospels*, such as the portraits of the four Evangelists.

The origin of the *Lindisfarne Gospels*

The Lindisfarne community sought a living memorial worthy of their beloved Cuthbert, but entirely for the glory of God. The *Lindisfarne Gospels* were this memorial. They were inscribed over a period some time between Cuthbert's death in 687 and the death of the scribe, Bishop Eadfrith, in 721.

After his death on the Inner Farne, Cuthbert's body was buried at Lindisfarne. His tomb became the focus of major pilgrimages, and healings took place there. Janet Backhouse, who until 1998 was the Curator of Illuminated Manuscripts at what is now the British Library, thought that the monks decided after 11 years that they should 'elevate' his remains and place them in a more glorious shrine on the anniversary of his death, 20 March. Some assumed that the *Lindisfarne Gospels* were dedicated and used for the first time on the same day. Michelle Brown, who succeeded Backhouse, postulates that the *Gospels* were not finished until the death of Eadfrith, since there are indications that they were not quite complete at this time.

The making of the *Gospels*

Our knowledge of the date and origin of the *Lindisfarne Gospels* rests with a colophon, added some 250 years later by a monk at Durham named Aldred.

The Gospels were written in Latin, the then living language of church worship. Aldred translated the Latin into Anglo-Saxon by writing between the lines in his own hand – the earliest example of Old English. At the end he added this colophon:

> Eadfrith, Bishop of Lindisfarne, wrote this book, at the first, in honour of God and St Cuthbert and all the saints in common who are on the island. And Ethilwald, Bishop of Lindisfarne, bound it on the outside and covered it, as he was well able to do. And Billfrith, the Anchorite, wrought the ornaments on the outside and adorned it, this unalloyed metal guilded over, with gold and gems and also with silver.

It is often assumed that Billfrith made a separate outer case, of the kind used for more valuable Irish manuscripts, such as for *Molaise's Gospels* which is now in the National Museum in Dublin. The meaning of the final part of the colophon is not entirely clear. It possibly means that Aldred earned for himself a home in the Durham monastery, the Community of Saint Cuthbert, by his work. He dedicated the first part (Saint Matthew) to God and Saint Cuthbert, the second part (Saint Mark) to his bishop, and the third (Saint Luke) to his brothers who were custodians of the shrine. He did the work on Saint John for himself, with the hope that he would gain admission to heaven!

All we know for certain of Aldred is that he was the son of Alfred and 'a good woman' named Tilwin.[19] Some have

19. From a note by Aldred at the end of the *Gospels*.

assumed that he was the same Aldred who was Bishop of Durham (that is, Chester-le-Street) from 957–968.

The Vikings and the Monks' Journey

In 793, the first of 200 years of Viking raids destroyed the Lindisfarne monastery, but not the shrine of Saint Cuthbert. In 875, according to the *Anglo-Saxon Chronicles*, the Danes ravaged Lindisfarne and 'destroyed all the monasteries.' The Chronicles also say that 'Eardulf, bishop of Lindisfarne, and abbot Eadred, taking the body of Saint Cuthbert from the island of Lindisfarne, wandered about for seven years'.[20] A succession of brothers carried Cuthbert, the symbol of the Church of the Northumbrians. Theirs was a church of a people – the Northumbrians – not of a place. Fenwick Lawson's magnificent sculpture of six monks carrying the enshrined body of Saint Cuthbert is named 'The Journey', and etches this epic journey in many visitors' minds. (The original in wood is at Saint Mary's Lindisfarne, and a bronze copy is in Durham's Millennium Square.) For years those monks walked from place to place, seeking God's guidance as to where they should stop. Cuthbert's Cave, at Holborn, near Belford, is by tradition the nearest stopping place to Lindisfarne.

The only authority for the history of the manuscript from this time is Symeon of Durham, who wrote early in the twelfth century. He states that Bishop Eardulph and Eadred, Abbot of Luel (Carlisle), were acting upon Cuthbert's final instructions when they removed his enshrined body to the mainland. In Cuthbert's shrine were also placed the most

20. The *Anglo-Saxon Chronicles* is a collection of annals in Old English chronicling the history of the Anglo-Saxons. The original manuscript of the *Chronicles* was created late in the ninth century.

valued relics. These included the bones of Eadbert and Ethilwald. Oswald's head had already been placed there, as most likely had some of Aidan's bones. Finally the *Lindisfarne Gospels* themselves were secured within it.

Symeon records the legend that Eardulph, Eadred and Lindisfarne brothers initially went to the Solway Firth in an attempt to sail to Ireland, but they met with a sudden storm. He writes:

> In this storm, while the ship was lying over on her side, a copy of the Gospels, adorned with gold and precious stones, fell overboard and sank into the depths of the sea. Accordingly, after a little while, when they had in some degree recovered their senses and reflected who and where they were, they bend their knees and prostrate themselves at full length before the feet of the sacred body, asking pardon for their foolish venture. Then they seize the helm and turn the ship back to the shore.[21]

After seeing a vision, a man named Hunred told them to wait for the low tide and then search for the lost manuscript. The sea had, unusually, receded three miles. They walked this distance and discovered the manuscript. To their amazement it retained all its glory, as if it had never been touched by water. It was possibly at this time that the covers were lost.

Stopping places during the seven years of wanderings may have included Melrose. After these seven years, the shrine appears to have remained for four months at Craike in Yorkshire, in 883, and that same year the Lindisfarne see was re-established at Chester-le-Street where the shrine rested

21. Rollason, David, (ed), *Symeon of Durham* (Oxford: Oxford Medieval Texts, 2000).

until 995. At this time it was transferred to Ripon by Bishop Aldhun to escape renewed invasions.

Only two months later they had to leave Ripon. Legend has it that at some point on the monks' journey back to Chester-le-Street with the body of Saint Cuthbert, the cart carrying the coffin suddenly stopped and could not be moved. The leader of the community, Bishop Aldhun, had a vision of Saint Cuthbert demanding to be taken to a place called 'Dunholme', but nobody knew where it was.

The puzzled monks stood perplexed as to how they would find Dunholme. Then a cow girl walked by and asked another young woman if she had seen a lost dun (brown) cow. The young woman said she had seen the cow heading in the direction of Dunholme – and pointed the way. The monks, who had overheard this exchange, decided to follow the cow girl, and found that Saint Cuthbert's coffin moved readily in that direction. They continued along that road and arrived in Dunholme (Durham).[22]

Durham

There were several factual reasons for Saint Cuthbert's community to have chosen Durham. Like many Anglo-Saxon priests, the community's leader, Bishop Aldhun, was married. His daughter was married to Uchtred, who had become the Earl of Northumbria. As a dowry, Aldhun had

22. Various intelligent guesses have been made as to the stopping places. In 1828, James Raine proposed Lindisfarne, Elsdon, Bellingham, Bewcastle, Salkeld, Mouth of the River Derwent, up the coast to Whithorn (seeking, then finding the lost *Gospels*), Carlisle, Cotherstone, Marske, Forsett, Crayke Abbey, Chester-le-Street (from 883 until 995), Ripon, Watden Law, and Durham, arriving 997. Professor David Rollason gave a much less detailed suggestion based on their presumed use of the Roman road system. In 2006, Teesdale Record Society Journal printed an unattributed piece of research entitled 'St. Cuthbert's Journey: The Stuff of Legend or the Victim of Unrecorded Fact'. Like a detective novel, and using both local tradition and Google Earth technology, it produced a much more detailed list of stopping places in a seven-stage journey.

received extensive land for the Church, which included Durham. For people seeking a safe haven from raids, Durham, a peninsula protected by a river with very steep banks, was ideal.

The community's move to Durham was beneficial from the point of view of Uchtred as well – it would provide a reason, and perhaps the finances, for the construction of a defensive complex. In addition, Saint Cuthbert would bring tremendous prestige and, through continuous pilgrimage, prosperity.

The Christian community of Cuthbert overthrew anti-Christian Vikings and helped to install Guthred as ruler. This gave Alfred, King of Wessex and many of the southern regions of the English, a good person to negotiate with. Alfred made peace with Guthred, baptised him and became his godfather. In 934, Alfred's grandson, King Athelstan, visited Cuthbert's shrine. These events are often seen as the making of a unified England.

At first, a small wattle church was erected, to be replaced in due course by the present cathedral, which still houses Saint Cuthbert's shrine at the east end. We know that the *Gospels* remained in Durham until at least the twelfth century, but their subsequent history remains a mystery. They are generally thought to have been returned to Lindisfarne, which was refounded at the end of the eleventh century as a daughter priory of the Durham Benedictine Community of Saint Cuthbert; it is the remains of this priory that visitors to Lindisfarne see today. An inventory of Lindisfarne of the year 1367 refers to a book of Saint Cuthbert.

In 1534, King Henry VIII ordered that monasteries be dissolved. No one knows what happened to the *Gospels* at that time; perhaps a devout landowner became their purchaser or custodian. They were eventually acquired by Sir Robert Cotton, either directly or indirectly, from Robert Bowyer, Keeper of the Records in the Tower and Clerk of the Parliaments under James I. The book was rebound in its present covers in 1853 at the expense of Dr Edward Maltby, Bishop of Durham. Cotton's library came to the British Museum in the eighteenth century, and from there to the British Library in London when this was separated from the British Museum.

Before the dawn of the third millennium, the Lindisfarne Centre opened on Holy Island – its centrepiece is a superb digital version of the *Lindisfarne Gospels* with interactive activities – and the *Lindisfarne Gospels Garden* opened opposite. At around the same time, the Lindisfarne Scriptorium, a small business run by Mary Fleeson, opened nearby. It takes its spiritual and visual inspiration from the work of the monks who created the *Lindisfarne Gospels* and the *Book of Kells*. The calligraphy, illumination and illustration it offers is a merging of old skills with new materials and new techniques inspired by ancient sacred works. The Scriptorium aims to offer an art form which draws the viewer into an experience of prayer, meditation and blessing. Each print from the Scriptorium has the following quote from Mary with it: 'We aim to follow the great Monastic Scriptorium tradition of producing pieces of artwork that give glory to God and help his people to worship.'

Monks travelling from Iona to Lindisfarne via the Firth of Forth are likely to have stopped off at Aberlady, a place that facilitated cultural and economic exchange. Among many Anglo-Saxon finds is a fragment of an eighth-century high cross which depicts artwork from the *Lindisfarne Gospels*.

These finds suggest that there was a major monastic settlement there. The high cross has recently been reconstituted and now stands proudly in the Kirk graveyard and heritage site. A Saint Aidan's Way pilgrimage route from Aberlady to Lindisfarne is now being promoted.

Durham Cathedral also promotes a digital version of the *Gospels*. In November 2011, British and international artists took part in the UK's largest light festival, whose most stunning installation encased Durham Cathedral in pages from the *Gospels*.

The return of the *Gospels* to the north for their 1300th anniversary celebrations in 2013 has led campaigners to call for a permanent refocusing of the *Gospels* which would give them a more worthy place at the heart of British culture. Ideas include placing sculptured reproductions in Westminster or Trafalgar Square, using the real *Gospels* in future coronations, incorporating annual celebrations in the Church calendar, and using them as a tool for meditation and spiritual and cultural renewal.

3. The strands of the *Lindisfarne Gospels*

(a) The Egyptian strand – the ascetic

One of the earliest known Gospel books in Celtic lands, the *St Cuthbert Gospel*, is bound and sewn in a specifically Coptic manner, which Michelle Brown believes indicates 'an actual learning/teaching process' linking Egypt and Northumbria.[23] The sewing enabled the pages to be opened wide for ease of reading, though it was not suitable for hard-bound copies that were reserved for occasional use, such as the *Lindisfarne Gospels*.

By the mid eighth century it had become the practice to adorn the opening of each of the Gospels in an illuminated manuscript with a page depicting the Gospel author (the Evangelist) and his symbol, and with another page known as the 'carpet page'. Carpet pages are wholly devoted to ornamentation with brilliant colours, active lines and complex patterns of interlace. The earliest surviving example of a carpet page is from the early seventh century *Bobbio Orosius*, and relates more closely to Late Antique decoration. There are notable carpet pages in the *Book of Kells*, the *Book of Durrow* and other manuscripts.

Some art historians find the origin of carpet pages on similar Coptic decorative book pages.[24] The carpet pages of the *Lindisfarne Gospels* are inspired by Coptic work, usually arranged around the shape of a cross and largely sticking to the 'Coptic palette' of greens and reds, combined with local

---

23. Brown, Michelle, *The Lindisfarne Gospels: Society, Spirituality and the Scribe*, p.206.
24. See, for example, Calkins, Robert G., *Illuminated Books of the Middle Ages* (New York: Cornell University Press, 1983).

innovations such as the interwound necks and wings of the gannets the artist would have seen from his cell.

A Christian community existed at Ruthwell, near the north-western border of Northumbria. The flower of its artistic achievements is the Ruthwell Cross, which is usually dated to the eighth century. It includes poetry from 'the Caedmon school' (named after the cowherd at Saint Hilda's Whitby monastery who composed poetic Bible songs in the English language at the time of Cuthbert). From their studies of Ruthwell, scholars suggest that its art reflects not only Roman innovations but also a strong interest in the monastic movement of Coptic Egypt. There is a panel showing the two greatest Desert Fathers – Saint Paul the hermit with Saint Anthony of Egypt, the first monk – breaking bread in their cave. Likewise, on the front of the Cross is an image of Christ which Ernst Kitzinger has compared to a panel in Saint Catherine's monastery in the Sinai. Christ is shown receiving the submission of the beasts of the earth in the desert, as the accompanying inscription records: *bestiae et dracones cognoverunt in deserto salvatorem mundi* – 'the beasts and dragons knew in the desert the Saviour of the World'.

Certainly the early monks of Britain and Ireland consciously regarded Saint Antony of Egypt as their ideal and their prototype, an inspiration that was acknowledged by contemporaries. In a letter to Charlemagne, the Northumbrian scholar Alcuin of York described the Irish monks as 'pueri Egyptiaci' ('the children of the Egyptians'). The proudest boast of Celtic monasticism was that, in the words of the *Antiphonary of Bangor*:

> This house full of delight
> Is built on the rock
> And indeed the true vine
> Transplanted out of Egypt.[25]

Egyptian pottery – perhaps originally containing wine or olive oil – has been found during excavations at Tintagel Castle in Cornwall, while the Litany of Irish Saints remembers 'the seven monks of Egypt [who lived] in Disert Uilaig' on the west coast of Ireland.[26] Travel guides in circulation in early Christian Britain gave accounts of the Egyptian monasteries. One of the earliest leaders of the Anglo-Saxon church was the Byzantine Theodore of Tarsus, sent to be Archbishop of Canterbury from his home in what is now southern Turkey.

In his *New York Review of Books* essay entitled 'The Egyptian Connection', William Dalrymple writes:

> Contrary to the impression given by earlier generations of scholars such as Henri Pirenne, the Islamic conquest of the Near East does not seem to have brought an end to this contact. The Anglo-Saxon Saint Willibald left an account of his visit in the 720s to the monastery of Mar Saba in Palestine where Saint John Damascene was then writing his refutation of heresies entitled *The Fount of Knowledge.* This contains a detailed critique of Islam, the first ever written by a Christian, in which Damascene regarded Islam essentially as Christian heresy related to Arianism and Monothelitism, which the Ruthwell sculptor was so concerned to avoid.
>
> What makes this link so intriguing is that Michelle Brown demonstrates convincingly how the same Coptic and Eastern

25. The *Antiphonary of Bangor* is an ancient Latin manuscript, supposed to have been originally written at Bangor Abbey.
26. Plummer, Charles (ed.), *Irish Litanies: Text and Translation* (Henry Bradshaw Society) Vol. LXII.

Christian manuscripts that influenced the *Lindisfarne Gospels* also influenced the work of early Islamic painters and calligraphers. The fascinating point that emerges from her book is that, to a considerable extent, both the art and sacred calligraphy of Anglo-Saxon England and that of the theology of the Desert Fathers was deeply austere, with much concentration on judgement and damnation, a concern that they passed on to the Irish monks:

> The space of air is choked by a wild mass
> of [Satan's] treacherous attendants . . .
> The day of the Lord, most righteous King of Kings, is at hand:
> a day of anger and vindication, of darkness and of cloud . . .
> a day also of distress, of sorrow and sadness,
> in which the love and desire of women will cease
> and the striving of men, and the desire of this world.

There is much in the [Quran] – notably its graphic hell scenes and emphasis on Godly Judgement – that, though off-putting to many modern Western readers, would have been quite familiar both to a Desert Father and a monk on Iona. Today many commentators in the US and Europe view Islam as a religion very different from and indeed hostile to Christianity.

Yet in their roots the two are closely connected, the former growing directly out of the latter and still, to this day, embodying many early Christian practices lost in Christianity's modern Western incarnation.

Just as the Celtic monks used prayer carpets for their devotions, so the Muslim form of prayer with its prostrations derives from the older Eastern Christian tradition that is still practised today in pewless churches across the Levant. The Sufi Muslim tradition carried on directly from the point at which the Desert Fathers left off, while Ramadan is in fact nothing more than an Islamicisation of Lent, which in the

> Eastern Christian churches still involves a gruelling all-day fast. Likewise, the recent outbreak of iconoclasm seen in Taliban Afghanistan had many counterparts in Christian history: the Ruthwell Cross was itself broken down and briefly buried as recently as the seventeenth century after the General Assembly of the Church of Scotland passed an Act ordering 'the demolishing of Idolatrous Monuments'.
>
> Certainly if a monk from seventh-century Lindisfarne or Egypt were to come back today it is probable that he would find much more that was familiar in the practices and beliefs of a modern Muslim Sufi than he would with, say, a contemporary American evangelical. Yet this simple truth has been lost by our tendency to think of Christianity as a Western religion, rather than the thoroughly Oriental faith it actually is. Because of this, we are apt to place Celtic monks, Coptic Desert Fathers, and Muslim Sufis in very different categories. But as the art of this period so clearly demonstrates, we are wrong to do so. These apparently different worlds were all surprisingly closely interlinked; indeed in intellectual terms perhaps more so in the eighth century than in today's nominally globalised world.[27]

The ascetic Egyptian Desert Fathers became known as Athletes of Christ because they stripped themselves of unnecessary accretions and ceaselessly trained to defeat destructive passions. Their gift to us is spiritual fitness.

(b) The Byzantine strand – the timeless

When the city of Rome fell to pagan invaders in 410, Jerome exclaimed, 'The renowned city, the capital of the Roman Empire, is swallowed up.'[28] The capital of the Empire

27. Dalrymple, William, 'The Egyptian Connection', *New York Review of Books*, 23 October 2008.
28. Jerome, 'Letter CXXVIII to Gaudentius', quoted in Schaff, P. (ed), *Jerome: The Principal Works of St Jerome* (http://www.ccel.org/ccel/schaff/npnf206.iv.II.html. Accessed 21 January 2013).

transferred to Christian Byzantium – today's Istanbul. The universal church was as yet undivided so naturally, as far as the restricted routes of communication allowed, influences of Christian thought and art were shared.

Michelle Brown thinks that woven into the pages of the *Lindisfarne Gospels* are testimonies to the learning and culture of early Byzantium as well as of other cultures.[29] The portraits of the Evangelists Matthew and Luke feature the bearded figures of Byzantine art which have become familiar to us in icons. In the Matthew portrait, a curtain is drawn aside: this is a feature that has become familiar to us in icons as symbolising a glimpse into eternity. The Gospel writers are portrayed as scribes as they are in Byzantine art.

Brown thinks that the cross upon a shaft or column may be of Byzantine derivation, and that the display captioning of the portraits of the four Evangelists, the angular capitals and syllabic layout, the figural forms of the frescoes and icons are reminiscent of Byzantium as well as of Rome:

> These influences are not surprising, for the sea trade routes to Byzantium remained open, and researchers have ascertained that some of the pigments and other artists materials used in Gospel illumination were imported from as far as Byzantium.[30]

John the Evangelist, who is depicted with an eagle in the *Lindisfarne Gospels*, as in other Gospels, went to live in the Byzantine region that is now Turkey. Many visit the house in which he is supposed to have lived in Ephesus.

In speaking of the dating of Easter, Bede reports the words of Bishop Colman at the Synod of Whitby that 'it is the same which the blessed John the Evangelist, the disciple

---

29. Brown, *The Lindisfarne Gospels: Society, Spirituality and the Scribe*, p.1.
30. Ibid., pp.323, 326.

specially beloved of our Lord, with all the churches over which he presided, is recorded to have celebrated'. Bede also tells us that 'a greater controversy [had arisen] about the observance of Easter, and *other rules of ecclesiastical life*'.[31]

It is a tendency of communities to take not only the detail of rituals but the greater dogmas from those in whom they vest the origins of their beliefs and practices. So if Colman saw the Celtic heritage in Johannine terms, it should not surprise us that this is reflected in the Gospels that were written in honour of Cuthbert, who chose to study John's Gospel with his mentor Boisil during the last week of Boisil's life.

Some would argue that the Columban Irish instinctively embraced a Johannine understanding of the Gospel with its emphasis on the Trinity, servanthood and relationship.

More than two centuries later, Vladimir, the Prince of Kiev, capital of ancient Russia, sent messengers to search the world for a religion that the rising Russian state could adopt. Eventually they entered the great Hagia Sophia cathedral in Byzantium. They reported to the Prince that with the sublime beauty of the singing and in the domed building they could not tell if they were in heaven or on earth. The Russians became Eastern Orthodox Christians. This timeless affinity with heaven on earth, reflected in icons and worship alike, is perhaps Byzantium's greatest gift to the world.

(c) The Roman strand – the order

Brown suggests that the display script in the *Gospels* reflects an Italian style, as does the depiction of Mark as a young, clean-shaven man. By the time of Aidan's seventh-century

31. Bede, *The Ecclesiastical History*, Book 3 chapter 25.

Lindisfarne monastery, the Church in Rome had regained influence as a centre for teaching, administration and resources. Gregory became an outstanding head of the city's civil administration.

During this period, Columba had a strategy meeting with Kentigern, Bishop of Strathclyde, as they were so concerned about the incursions of paganism among the Britons, from the Picts in the north and the invading Angles and Saxons from the east. Following that meeting, Kentigern visited Gregory and most likely asked for support. Gregory would have been sympathetic. We have already noted that, upon seeing Angle boys being sold as slaves in Rome he had said, 'They are not Angles, but angels.'[32] Gregory became a monk and was promptly made pope. Pope Gregory sent a small delegation to Iona and a large mission team to Kent in 597.

The Kent mission sent Bishop Paulinus to preach in Northumbria, because Kent's Princess Ethelberg agreed to become the queen of Northumbria's pagan King Edwin only on condition that he allowed this. It seems to have been more like a firework display than a lasting fire. Bede reports that when Edwin was slain, the thousands who had been baptised returned to their pagan gods. However, it seems unlikely that the Christian King Oswald would have been accepted as the chief of the English kings if he had not made some attempts to connect with kingdoms which followed the Roman tradition. Some scholars suggest that he sustained a royal church at York which reflected some of the Roman decoration and customs, in contrast to the simple wooden constructs that Aidan preferred at Lindisfarne.

The significant connection between Lindisfarne and the Roman tradition came through another Kent princess who

32. Bede, *The Ecclesiastical History* Book 2 chapter 1.

married a Northumbrian king – Enfleda, wife of Oswy. In the late 640s she sponsored Wilfrid, who loved all things Roman, to become a student at the by now prestigious monastery school at Lindisfarne. Her insistence on keeping to the Roman dates for Easter was the ostensible trigger for the 664 Synod of Whitby, which decided to adopt Roman customs. The date of Easter and the form of monastic tonsure were two separate issues, but many other customs were also changed. We may deduce this from the fact that the Lindisfarne monks who did not emigrate to Ireland complained to their new prior, Cuthbert, about one thing after another!

When Eadfrith knew he was going to write the *Lindisfarne Gospels*, he visited the monastery at Jarrow, which contained many books from Rome. He borrowed a copy of the Gospels, which had probably come from Naples. It used the Latin version of the Bible, known as the Vulgate, which Pope Damasus commissioned Jerome to produce in 382. The 16 pages of canon tables, although decorated with a Celtic style of ornament, owe their style of framing to the late classical form that was prevalent in Italy and in Greek-speaking areas of the Roman Empire. The canon tables were a simple form of concordance, devised by Eusebius of Caesarea, in which the Gospels are divided into numbered sections and parallel sections from other Gospels are cross-referenced.

The reason a pope asked Jerome to produce a Bible in the 'vulgar tongue' – that is, in the Latin that ordinary people spoke – was so that the Church should not fragment. Its Scriptures, as also its Creeds, its calendar and its clerical organisation needed coherence, and therefore order. Something of that order is reflected in the *Lindisfarne Gospels*.

(d) The Irish strand – the human

Throughout the world the Irish are loved, not for their organisation or order, but for their humour and warm hearts.

We have seen how the Irish missionary Aidan refused either to dominate or demean people, or to put on airs. It was his authenticity that drew people to him and his way of life. When King Oswin remonstrated with him for giving away to a beggar the expensive royal horse he had given for Aidan's use, Aidan said to the king, 'Which is more precious to you, that son of a mare or (referring to the beggar) that son of God?'[33]

If other strands of Christianity are best represented by angular shapes such as the square, the Irish strand is best represented by the inclusive, primal circle and by interlacing curves that need never to be cut and chopped. The *Lindisfarne Gospels* are full of curvilinear patterns that bring the page to life. There are simple spirals and whorls where two lines enter the spiral from opposite directions. Some of these expand into different shapes such as a trumpet. The system has extraordinary flexibility. A particularly good example is the four panels of curves on the Saint Mark carpet page.

Flexibility, humanity, hospitality – how these gifts are needed today.

(e) The Celtic British strand– the wisdom

Michelle Brown writes that 'the design context for much of the *Lindisfarne Gospels* ornament therefore lies firmly within a British, Pictish and Celtic tradition which stretched back to the Iron Age and which was actively practised in those areas around and after the time that the volume was made'.[34]

33. Bede, *The Ecclesiastical History* (Oxford University Press), p.133.
34. Brown, *The Lindisfarne Gospels: Society, Spirituality and the Scribe*, p.296.

Rosemary Cramp points out that geometric aids in the Gospels, such as the pectoral cross and the Lindisfarne sculptures, form part of an ancient British and Celtic tradition.[35]

Although Bede, the main historian of seventh-century Northumbrian Christianity, tends to overlook the presence of the Christian Britons who continued to live in the area, Melrose, in whose monastery Cuthbert trained, is a British name, and it is possible that some of those who trained there, or indeed at Lindisfarne were 'British boys'.

In the eleventh century, a married priest in the Community of Cuthbert, which looked after Cuthbert's shrine at Durham, fathered Aelred, the Hexham monk who wrote *Lives* about saints Ninian (fifth century) and Kentigern (sixth and seventh century). Aelred clearly thought that these British apostles were a significant part of Northumbria's Christian birthright. As Northumbria expanded it embraced Whithorn, where Ninian established his great monastery of 'the Shining House', and to which, following the Viking invasions, Lindisfarne's monks briefly fled with their precious *Gospels.*

Kentigern, who founded the Christian church in what is now Glasgow, was forced into temporary exile. He went south in stages, gathering and preaching to people throughout that part of Northumbria that is now Cumbria, leaving behind small Christian groups.

Northumbria also briefly embraced Abernethy. As already indicated, legend has it that Nectan, king of the Picts, founded a church on the site of the present Church of Scotland in AD460 that was dedicated to Saint Brigid of

35. Cramp, R. J., 'The Artistic Influence of Lindisfarne Within Northumbria' in Bonner et al, *St Cuthbert, His Cult and His Community to AD 1200* (Boydell: 1989).

Ireland. It is recorded that the Picts' King Gartnaidh built the first stone church there around 590.

Abernethy lies north of the Firth of Forth. At the time of the *Gospels*, the Forth formed Northumbria's northern border. On the southern side of the Forth is Aberlady. Archeologists believe that a small church existed there before Aidan's mission arrived, and that his mission team would most likely have stopped there before journeying on to Bamburgh. In 1863, a fragment of an early Christian cross was found there. As already indicated, the carved designs are strikingly similar to illuminated artwork that characterises the *Lindisfarne Gospels.* The beautifully carved cross suggests a settlement of some significance, perhaps a monastic foundation.

Saint Hilda's father, Prince Hereric, a nephew of King Edwin, sought protection in the little Celtic (Brythonic) kingdom of Elmet when Edwin was ousted. However, someone poisoned him, and when Edwin regained his throne the following year (617), he conquered Elmet. It has been postulated that Hereric had links with Elmet through his wife, Hilda's mother, who may even have been a Briton herself.

During the century of the *Lindisfarne Gospels*, the indigenous British were rudderless, but they retained their beliefs. The Anglo-Saxons had destroyed their leadership, but not the entire infrastructure outside their fortified high grounds. Many of the Anglo-Saxon landowners would have had British peasants as labourers. What was their Christian folk memory and DNA?

Aidan's vast diocese included the Cymric speaking people who were still quite populous in Cumbria. These, like the Irish, would almost certainly have known stories of Saint

Patrick, their 'son', who perhaps went to school in Carlisle, and maybe even overlapped with Ninian before being captured by Irish slave traders. The evangelistic fervour and the battling prayers of this Briton who laid down his life to bring the Irish to Christ could not have perished from their hearts.

The Celtic Britons have been described as 'God intoxicated', yet the monk Gildas, in *The Ruin of Britain*, described a fifth and sixth century British Church that had become morally lax following the departure of the Romans.[36] This, however, was followed by a new wave of holiness. Illtyd founded a great monastic school at what is now Llantwit Major, to which a whole generation of future British church leaders came – Samson, Gildas, Dubricius (who also features in the Arthurian fables), David and Paulinus, to name but a few. The *Life of Samson* by Samson's nephew is perhaps the best historical source we have for these Christian Britons.[37]

It was said that Illtyd was the most learned of all Britons in the knowledge of the Old and New Testaments, philosophy, poetry, rhetoric, grammar and literature, not to mention agriculture, for he invented a vastly improved plough. Illtyd became known as 'the wisest of Britons', so, if we have to choose one word to describe Celtic British spirituality, perhaps 'wisdom' is the most appropriate.

(f) The Anglo-Saxon strand – the heroic

According to the ninth-century historian Nennius, the Saxons initially arrived in Britain with only 40 ships. The Saxon colonisation was not a case of mass invasion that

36. Winterbottom, Michael, *Gildas: The Ruin of Britain, and other works* (Phillimore, 1978).
37. Taylor, Thomas (trans), *The Life of Samson of Dol* (Llanerch Press).

replaced the indigenous population. The invaders were men, so in large part they must have taken their wives from the indigenous Celtic British population. The Saxons became the rulers because of their clarity, cohesion and courage. They made for hilltop settlements, commanded the heights and from these they extended their influence. They were fearless and well organised in battle. Their story of Beowulf has become familiar to modern audiences through new translations and film. This great warrior, famed for heroic feats, takes fellow warriors from his tribe to rescue the Danes, whose warriors have been decimated by the monster Grendel. Beowulf tears Grendel to pieces.

The UK's largest haul of Anglo-Saxon treasure was discovered buried in a Staffordshire field in 2009, probably the spoils of battle. The collection of 1500 gold and silver pieces, which probably date to the seventh century, is worth a huge amount and reveals the Anglo-Saxons' love of gold and quality artefacts. As the early pagan Anglo-Saxons had no books and were often on the move, their art was largely ornamental and non-representational, portable and small in scale. At its finest – such as is seen in the magnificent shoulder clasps and belt buckles found amid the grave goods of the pagan ship burial at Sutton Hoo, from the early seventh century – pagan Anglo-Saxon art was also fabulously intricate and lavish, with interwoven animal, interlace and checkerboard patterns formed of glass, garnets, enamel and – a particular feature of pagan Saxon work – solid gold.

According to Elizabeth Coatsworth, the design used for Saint Cuthbert's pectoral cross with its precise geometry based upon grids and compass-drawn circles was also used for the central motif of one of the *Lindisfarne Gospels'* carpet pages. She traces this tradition to items of Anglo-Saxon metalwork such as the Ixworth and Wilton crosses, and wonders whether the Gospels' illuminator was himself a metalworker.[38]

We still name Wednesday after Woden, the Saxon god of victory. When the Anglo-Saxons exchanged their gods for the Christian God, their heroic instinct was harnessed to a higher good; it was not neutered. The young King Oswald, following his breathtaking victory over Cadwallon's much larger forces, personified this. The most famous of Anglo-Saxon poems, an indirect fruit of Lindisfarne, is *The Dream of the Rood.* In this superb piece of Christian inculturation, the Christ who allows himself to be killed is portrayed as an Anglo-Saxon warrior. The Tree on which he was crucified declares:

> I remember the morning a long time ago that I was felled at the edge of the forest and severed from my roots.
> Strong enemies seized me,
> bade me hold up their felons on high, and made me a spectacle.
> Men shifted me on their shoulders and set me on a hill.
> Many enemies fastened me there. I saw the Lord of humankind hasten with such courage to climb upon me. I dared not bow or break there
> against my Lord's wish, when I saw the surface of the earth tremble.
> I could have felled all my foes, yet I stood firm. Then the young warrior, God Almighty, stripped himself, firm and unflinching. He climbed upon the cross, brave before many, to redeem humankind.[39]

38. Coatsworth, E. & Pinder, M., *The Art of the Anglo-Saxon Goldsmith, Fine Metalwork in England, its Practice and Practitioners* (Woodbridge, 2002).
39. Crossley-Holland, Kevin (trans), *The Anglo-Saxon World* (Boydell & Brewer, 1994).

Heroism against an enemy became a heroism of service. Perhaps the lion, the symbol of Saint Mark in the *Lindisfarne Gospels*, catches something of that heroic spirit.

Today, people in Latin countries often speak of 'the Anglo-Saxon nations' (which include the USA, Australasia and Britain) as a culture which puts competition and economic conquest before community: that is the unredeemed face of Anglo-Saxon culture. The unredeemed Anglo-Saxon is the English football hooligan. The redeemed Anglo-Saxon spearheads a heroism of service in the most needy areas at home and abroad. The many animals that crowd into the pages of the *Lindisfarne Gospels* were beloved equally of the Saxons and the Irish, and are a sign that bloody-minded brutality is not the complete picture of the Anglo-Saxon. Heroism and dedication, when harnessed to the common good, may benefit the world.

(g) The Oriental strand – prayer rhythms

The carpet pages of the *Gospels* remind us of the oriental and Islamic tradition. Islam impacted the Middle Eastern countries at the very time that the emerging English Church made contact with those countries. Early Islam drew from ascetic forms of Christianity that originated in the Byzantine Levant but whose influence spread both to the Celtic north as well as to the Arabian south. Michelle Brown points out that Northumbrian, Celtic and Byzantine monks all used to pray on decorated prayer carpets, known as oratorii, just as Muslim and certain Eastern Christian Churches have always done, and still do. She speculates how these prayer mats may have influenced the carpet pages of manuscripts such as the *Lindisfarne Gospels* as well as early Islamic sacred texts.[40]

40. Brown, *The Lindisfarne Gospels: Society, Spirituality and the Scribe*, p.321.

Around the year 327, the Empress Helena claimed to have found the True Cross in Jerusalem. This is the subject of the finest poem of Cynewulf, Bishop of Lindisfarne from 740 to 780. As a result of this development, the custom grew of Christians kneeling on a prayer mat before a cross and kissing it before receiving the Eucharist. The use in the *Lindisfarne Gospels* of pages decorated like a carpet in the shape of a cross may have been intended to evoke adoration of the Tree of Life and celebration of Eucharistic communion with God in creation.

In the sanctuary and the side chapel of Saint Mary's Church, Holy Island, are two carpets made by island women under the direction of Miss Kathleen Parbury which replicate two of the carpet pages of the *Lindisfarne Gospels.* Before the altar in the cellar chapel of Holy Island's Open Gate Retreat House is a small, thicker prayer mat, beautifully woven by Mollie Richards, which pilgrims may pick up and use in the way Muslims use their prayer mats.

I salute the many faithful Muslims who kneel on their prayer mats five times a day, at times dictated by the movement of the sun. The first, 'Fair prayer', starts with the rise of the white light in the east. The midday prayer starts after the sun passes its zenith. The afternoon prayer starts before the sun begins to turn orange. The fourth prayer is at sunset and the final prayer is at night. I am saddened that so few modern Christians pray in the daily rhythm of the sun, as did the first Christians and their fellow Jews.

Traditionally, three Jewish prayer services are recited daily:

1. *Shacharit* or *Shaharit* (שַׁחֲרִית), from the Hebrew *shachar* or *shahar* (שַׁחַר) 'morning light'.

2. *Mincha* or *Minha* (מִנְחָה), the afternoon prayers named for the flour offering that accompanied sacrifices at the Temple in Jerusalem.
3. *Arvit* (עַרְבִית) or *Ma'ariv* (מַעֲרִיב), from 'nightfall'.

According to the Talmud, prayer is a biblical commandment, and the Talmud gives two reasons why there are three basic prayers: to recall the daily sacrifices at the Temple in Jerusalem, and/or because each of the Patriarchs instituted one prayer: Abraham the morning, Isaac the afternoon and Jacob the evening. (Tractate Taanit 2a, in reference to Deuteronomy 11:13: 'loving the Lord your God, and serving him with all your heart and with all your soul.')

The early Christians continued this practice of daily prayer (Acts 2:42, 46; 3:1; 10:3, 9). The Didache (a book of teaching by the first post-apostles generation) urged Christians to pray three times a day along the lines of Jesus' teaching on prayer.[41] Early Irish Christians related the daily rhythm of prayer to that of the sun and the moon, but references in Adomnan's *Life of St Columba* suggest that they measured time in standard hours, perhaps by a candle or water device.

Could members of our churches start to make prayer mats? Could parish churches restore public daily prayer heralded by the ringing of a bell? Members of dispersed communities such as the Community of Aidan and Hilda[42] commit to daily times of prayer that broadly reflect the sun's rising, zenith and setting: can many more sign up to this? Such rhythms of prayer are reflected on the Holy Island of Lindisfarne. Many visitors say, 'If only we could take the

---

41. http://www.paracletepress.com/didache.html. Accessed 15 January 2013.
42. http://www.aidanandhilda.org. Accessed 15 January 2013.

island back with us.' We tell them that they can – if they make God their island.

(h) Weaving – an approach to diversity

The *Lindisfarne Gospels* express an approach to diversity that glories in the best from each tradition, but does not celebrate what is unacceptable in it. Not only the carpet pages, but the entire book is a multicoloured tapestry.

A Conservative British Prime Minister (Edward Heath) once referred to 'the unacceptable face of capitalism'.[43] Each of the traditions reflected in the *Gospels* sooner or later developed its own unacceptable face. One example comes from Bishop Wilfrid of the Roman tradition. The church-planting zeal of this nobleman's son and his espousal of the glories of Rome may be celebrated, but his pride and lack of respect for people of simpler tastes has no place in a divine paeon of praise. Hexham Abbey celebrates Wilfrid as its patron, yet I heard the Dean of Hexham, in a sermon to the Sisters of the Order of the Holy Paraclete at Whitby, confess that Wilfrid's insistence that nine priests carry him bodily on a throne was 'over the top'!

The Way of Life of the international Community of Aidan and Hilda states: 'We seek to weave together the God-given strands of spirituality that have become separated.' Michael Mitton, a founder of that Community, writes in *Restoring the Woven Cord*, 'Our quest is to see the strands of our Christian faith once again woven into a strong cord so that the church at every level might be renewed by the power of the Holy Spirit.'[44]

43. House of Commons debate 4 August 1976. http://hansard.millbanksystems.com/commons/1976/aug/04/lonrho. Accessed 22 January 2013.
44. Mitton, Michael, introduction to *Restoring the Woven Cord: Strands of Celtic Christianity for the Church Today* (BRF, 2009).

To celebrate Pope Benedict 16th's visit to Scotland in 2011, a Saint Ninian's Day parade took place along Edinburgh's Royal Mile. The Pope and other visiting dignitaries were draped in blankets of Scottish tartan. The Duke of Edinburgh was overheard to quip, 'Have they got tartan knickers?' Was this an uncalled-for lewd joke or a piece of shrewd insight into the true basis of inculturation? Do cross-cultural missionaries take local culture into their inmost parts or merely put on a superficial image for a quick photo shot?

The 2012 London Olympic Games were widely regarded as 'happy and glorious'. No small part of this was due to the fact that athletes of the host country, 'Team GB', came from every ethnic background imaginable, rejoicing to be together, knowing that the sum was greater than the parts. The Church must now take its cue from that Olympic experience. We must surely expect to find among churches Caribbean bands and African chant, Byzantine iconography and Muslim-style prayer, western pop music and Gregorian plainsong, creation celebration, prophetic voices and social service, desert retreats and spiritual fitness courses. We must not despise or distance these different expressions; rather, like the *Lindisfarne Gospels*, we must weave them together in a glorious and attractive tapestry. Or, in the words of Rowan Williams, we must foster a 'mixed economy church'.

4. The spirituality of the *Lindisfarne Gospels*

(a) Illumination for us – Lectio Divina with these *Gospels*

Michelle Brown observes that a time and motion study of the duration it would have taken to complete the *Lindisfarne Gospels* might suggest that the task was given to an anchorite for whom the work was the prayer, and who was therefore granted exemption from some other duties. The act of copying and transmitting the *Gospels*, these 'portals of prayer', was to glimpse the divine and may have been a service offered on behalf of the community. She proposes an analogy between the work of the artist-scribe on such a spiritually charged project as the *Lindisfarne Gospels* and the desert ascetic who struggled with demons on behalf of the wider community, as did Cuthbert on the Inner Farne Isle. Both are sustained feats of spiritual and physical endurance as part of the apostolic mission to bring God's Word to the furthest outposts.[45]

Michelle Brown asks whether 'literacy' should be seen as the ability to interpret a range of signs and images and retain a coherent body of cultural memory.[46] She reminds us of the patristic concept of the 'inner library' and the necessity for each believer to make themselves a library of God's word, which Aidan's Irish colleague Cummian referred to as 'entering the Sanctuary of God'. The purpose of the artist-scribe was to illumine, both physically and spiritually, the meaning of the Divine word.

45. Brown, *The Lindisfarne Gospels: Society, Spirituality and the Scribe*, p.298.
46. Brown, Michelle, introduction to *The Book and the Transformation of Britain c. 550-1050: a Study in Written and Visual Literacy and Orality* (British Library, 2012).

Several themes of these illuminations ignite a glow within us as we contemplate them. The bright trumpet blasts and bursts of colour invoke within us a sense that we may celebrate Christ at the heart of all life. The carpet pages, shaped to remind us of wayside high crosses, call us to live life as a sacrificial journey. The fun-loving galaxy of dogs and birds who fit themselves in almost everywhere inspire us to enjoy God's sense of fun and the divine presence in creation. The geometric style, resonant of Muslim art which, fearing to make an idol of anything, points to God as Mystery beyond our fashioning, and the writing style, from Ireland, calls us to pursue excellence and do all things well.

There are 45 colours in the pages of the *Gospels*. A useful exercise is to ask what each colour says to us. Red reminds us of blood and of passion, green of life, and so on, but each colour may evoke a distinctive emotion in different individuals.

Reflecting with the *Lindisfarne Gospels*

Dr Jane Hawkes, Lecturer in Art History at York University, speaking at Laing Gallery, Newcastle, in November 2000 said of the *Lindisfarne Gospels*:

> Its art also invokes the art of leading the reader through the text; how art is used to draw out the sacred meaning of the words.

So we suggest that the ancient art of Lectio Divina is applied to the *Lindisfarne Gospels* which include both text and illuminations. The four stages of Lectio Divina are: 1) Lectio (reading) – the slow, faith-filled reading of a passage from the Gospels; 2) Meditatio (meditation) – thoughtful reflection upon what has been read; 3) Oratio (prayer) – a fervent prayer of dedication prompted by the reflection; 4) Contemplatio (contemplation) – silent communing with and enjoyment of God.

Christians in recent years have become familiar with Lectio Divina, or godly reading, and reflection upon the sacred text of Scripture. I believe that a double blessing can come from doing this with the illuminated *Gospels* open before us, for symbols as well as words have power to evoke devotion and inspire understanding. The apostle Paul describes us as 'God's masterpiece', that is, a work of art in the making (Ephesians 2:10, NLT). Meditation on these illuminated *Gospels* inspires us, like the artist-scribe, to give 'our utmost for God's highest', until 'the glory of God is seen in a human who is fully alive' (Irenaeus).[47] The next section, 'praying with the Evangelists', will offer a way of doing this.

Various popular editions of the *Lindisfarne Gospels* are available.[48] Unless you can read the Latin text of these *Gospels* or the early English translation handwritten between the text, open a modern translation of the passage you have chosen to read and place it beside the *Lindisfarne Gospels.*

First, read the text of the passage slowly. Visualise the scene. Ask questions such as: What did Jesus feel as he said or did this? What did others feel? How were they changed? If I was there, what question would I ask Jesus? What might Jesus say to me? Now, *look* at the page in the *Lindisfarne Gospels.* What comes to mind as you look at the beautiful script, or one of the decorations? Look at a facing page of decoration, where there is one. What do you feel? What do you imagine? What impulse moves you?

Write down your reflections. End with a prayer.

---

47. St Irenaeus, *Against Heresies*, Book IV, chapter 20. http://www.newadvent.org/fathers/0103420.htm. Accessed 22 January 2013.
48. One example is *The World of the Lindisfarne Gospels* by Michelle P. Brown (British Library, 2004). The illuminated pages can be found online, for example at http:/www.bl.uk/onlinegallery/ttp/lindisfarne/accessible/introduction.html.

(b) The four Evangelists – archetypes for a fully human spirituality

A tool used by pioneers of authentic spirituality is the four archetypes, drawn from the work of C. G. Jung. Jung has observed that 'Our symbols explain the world around us, our relationships with each other and our relationship to the universe. These symbols, these essences of pure being, are the primordial qualities of the truly real.'[49]

Four archetypes that are increasingly used as a basis for meditation by Christian mentors are the Warrior, Magus (Shaper), Lover and King. Spirituality coaches such as Fr Richard Rohr relate these archetypes to aspects of Christ. Each of the four Gospel writers portrays a distinctive aspect of Christ. In art, each of these four Evangelists is represented by a symbol. The symbols are drawn from two visions: that of the Old Testament prophet Ezekiel (10:11) and that of the New Testament Book of Revelation (4:7). They found their way into illustrations of the Gospels from early centuries, including the *Lindisfarne Gospels.*

I have found that the method known as Lectio Divina, widely used for reflecting on the text of the Gospels, may also be used to reflect on the symbols. Before the text of each Gospel in the *Lindisfarne Gospels* is a page which introduces us, in visual form, to its author. The *Gospels* are the first such book in Britain and Ireland to portray the human author. Open this page and meditate upon it.

In the following notes for meditation, I have related each of the four portraits to one of the four archetypes. Christ lived each of the archetypes to the full. One archetype was

49. Jung, Carl G., *Archetypes and the Collective Unconscious* (London, 1996).

perhaps more dominant than others in each of the four Evangelists. Reflection on each of them therefore offers us a tool whereby we may live each of the archetypes more fully.

Have open before you the portrait of the Evangelist Mark (see page 142) and take time to do the following meditation. Look at the appropriate portrait for each of the four Archetype meditations.

The Warrior (Mark)

The warrior is always alert, focused and clear thinking. He accepts that he may soon die, so he lives each moment to the full. The warrior is fit for purpose: he uses all his energy and skill to maximum effect. This involves self-control and the ability to take initiative at the right moment. A warrior completes the task he is given. Every part of his being, all his energy, is expended.

The warrior in Jesus is seen in his all-out self-giving from the beginning of his life to his last breath – and beyond it. The purpose of his birth, trials, teachings, signs, death, resurrection, ascension and sending of the Holy Spirit is that three evils may be overcome by good: sin, death and the devil. This seamless victory procession is known in Latin as Christus Victor. 'He has destroyed every ruler and every authority and power' (1 Corinthians 15:24).

Mark portrays Jesus' miracles as battles to overcome the forces of evil. Sometimes, English Bible translators have emasculated the signs and sounds of the warrior that came from Jesus. Mark 7:31-37 describes how Jesus took hold of a deaf and dumb man and used touch and sign for the sake of the man who could not hear. But Mark highlights the fact that Jesus also made a noise which English translations call a sigh, but which in fact was more like the sharp intaking and releasing of breath of a power weightlifter. It took a lot of power. He gave all he'd got.

Ancient Britons and the Saxon invaders who became the English were fierce warriors. Archaeological finds from the sixth century of a number of single weapons in rivers have led some to suggest that when Celtic warriors were baptised, they would leave their weapons and other regalia in the water and come out to be reclothed as warriors for Jesus.

Oswald grew up as a warrior prince at the garrison of his father, Northumbria's merciless pagan king. After 17 years, the king who had seized his father's throne was killed, and another usurper marched to seize it. Since Oswald was the rightful heir, he, like Gideon in the Bible, took a small but dedicated band of warriors to confront the invader. The night before the battle, the late founder of Iona, Columba, assured Oswald in a dream that his cause was just and that his small force, though greatly outnumbered, would win the battle. Oswald asked his men to kneel in prayer on the battlefield. Following his victory, he renamed it 'Heaven's Field' and planted a large wooden cross in it. Oswald's whole life was shaped by the Lord's Prayer: 'Your kingdom come on earth as it is in heaven.'

The 'putting on armour' prayers, such as Saint Patrick's Breastplate, were familiar to those steeped in the Irish tradition, and they can inspire us, too:

> I arise today through a mighty power, the Holy Trinity.
> I arise today through Christ's power in his birth and in his baptism.
> His power in his dying, his rising from the tomb, and in his coming again.
>
> This day for our shield we call
> God's strength to direct us,

God's power to sustain us,
God's wisdom to guide us,
God's vision to light us.
This day for our shield we call
God's ear for our hearing,
God's word for our speaking,
God's hand to uphold us
God's forces to save us.[50]

Now gaze at the page in the *Lindisfarne Gospels* that portrays Mark. We notice that he is young, clean-shaven and strong, with curly black hair, and that his symbol is a lion. The warrior is a lion-heart. Mark's primary colour is red – he is passionate. His Gospel is short, pithy, to the point.

Some scholars think that Mark wrote what Peter told him – Peter, the action man who tried to walk on water and who cut off the ear of an officer sent to arrest Jesus; Peter, who was all out for Jesus but who had to learn attributes associated with the other archetypes. Why did Mark take to Peter? Peter did not fear to take the plunge, to say what he thought, to ask questions. As he matured, Peter became willing to be led to a place to which he wished not to go: the place of crucifixion. That is the ultimate warrior – to conquer fear of death and loss of 'control'.

There was nothing half-hearted about the big fisherman, nor about his younger apprentice, Mark. The temptations the warrior has to overcome include impatience, insensitivity, lack of thought.

The lion on this page is large, near, in full strength, and roaring. The trumpet that comes out of his mouth could almost be fire spurting from his nostrils. He has wings, like

50. Adam, David (a former vicar of Lindisfarne), opening pages of *Cry of the Deer* (SPCK Classics, 2009).

each of the symbolic creatures, but his wings lie on the body: it is physical energy that is most operative.

The Evangelist writes on a single page: he is writing a book-in-the-making, but the lion holds between its claws a book already completed. Around Mark's neck are two collars that look like rays of light. One ray points to the book in his left hand; the other to the page on which he is writing.

On this earth, we act out a script that at times seems to be already written for us. Sometimes this script is our genetic and home conditioning: our lives become little more than conditioned reflexes. But suppose we act out God's script for our life's journey? We have complete free will. If we make a mistake we can tear up the page and start again. Yet, as we look back with the eyes of eternity, we might realise that the book of our life was already in God's hands. Will we 'write', in our every thought and deed, only what is God's script for us?

The colours around the Evangelist are contrasting and bright. A warrior utilises all that is around him. He does not hide his colours.

Go all out, full colours flying.
If you feel something – do something.
Get to the nub of things.
Have the courage of your convictions.
Allow yourself to be led step by step.
If you flinch from something, abandon yourself to the Providence in the midst of raging waves.

The Shaper (Magus) – Matthew

The Shaper is the observer, the scholar, the prophet, the interpreter who scans the horizons and puts life's jigsaw pieces into a whole picture. There is nothing intrinsically unChristian about such a person. He pushes the right buttons at the right time in order to obtain good energy flows and good outcomes. This may take material forms (for example, electrics) or non-material forms (for example, prayer). The magus is the introvert who taps into his own deep wellsprings and into the collective unconscious. He may use music, poetry, ritual, nature or oratory to do these things. Temptations he has to overcome include dithering, undue withdrawal from social interaction, taking short cuts, and failure to patiently mentor apprentices step by step.

As we gaze at the portrait of St Matthew, we see a man of intellect: he has a long beard and a thoughtful posture. His head is bowed in concentration. His footstool is ethereal. He seeks to harness the forces of the Hebrew tradition and of intellectual worlds to the Gospel. This is why he includes so many Old Testament quotations. Matthew's robe is green. Green speaks of seeds being scattered and bearing fruit in different places, of roots in holy tradition. He has long hair and a beard and exudes the wisdom of the scribe.

His feet are covered to keep this old man warm – not for him to pit his flesh against the elements. He is ethereal, not red-blooded. His is the inner world of shapes, ideas and memory. Matthew is inventive, creative, voluminous in his writing (his is the longest Gospel). Like Saint Paul, he seeks to 'take every thought captive to obey Christ' (2 Corinthians 10:5). He is the connector.

Matthew's symbol, alone among the four Evangelists, is that of a human figure, drawing aside a curtain. The Magus, or Shaper, is in touch with unseen dimensions: in Christ heaven comes to earth.

This person has little spare flesh. His trumpet penetrates the veil between earth and heaven.

You who light with heaven's glory,
leaf and lake and cloud and star,
light the hearts of all to justice,
bring to faith those now afar.
Pour your tender love upon us,
you who fill both souls and space,
turn us into sons and daughters,
lifting up the human race.

Learn to be still.
Tap into the deep wellsprings of your inner thoughts and stored memories.

The Lover – John

The Lover is alive to his feelings, his senses and his primal hungers. Artificial boundaries mean little to him. He uses tender touch. He feels the pain of love and knows that it is part of love's power. He is real. He can be at home in his own body without shame. He can play and be at home with others without pretence. John is 'the loved disciple' who knew much about being a lover of Christ. John is the contemplative who gazed into the face of Christ, felt his heartbeat at the last supper, and became (to use a word from *The Carmina Gadelica*) the foster brother of Jesus when Jesus bequeathed him to his mother before he died on the cross.

Now gaze at the page in the *Lindisfarne Gospels* that portrays John.

The authors of the other three Gospels (known as the Synoptics) sit sideways, with legs crossed or knees touching. John sits in a full frontal position with feet apart and gazes straight ahead with fully open eyes and unfurrowed brows. His symbol, the eagle, was thought to be the only bird that could gaze directly into the sun without being blinded.

In contrast to the other three Evangelists, who use both hands to clasp a scroll or book, John keeps one hand free. Is his other hand over his heart, where the light within resides, or is it pointing to Jesus the Living Light? The auras of the other three are a monochrome shade plus a rim: John's aura glows with lighter and darker shades. It would be difficult to distract John – he is in another world.

John's inner garment is bright green, which perhaps speaks of the organic fertility of creation. He knows that from the divine word springs all created life (John 1:3); creation is an expression of the being, the love of God. His outer garment is crimson, which speaks of the nobility of suffering. Its hems speak of flashing light.

The eagle soars and sees. The eagle has a circle around its head: it flies straight into the presence of Christ whom St Patrick had entitled 'The True Sun'. John is not engaged in writing. He is close to Jesus, who, while he was on earth, never wrote a book. The eagle also, however, carries the Gospel, the Book of Life.

I muse on the eternal Logos of God, and all creation is lit up.
I muse on the eternal Light, and every person is lit up.
I muse on the eternal Life, and God's heaven is lit up.
I muse on the beloved disciple at the Last Supper, and God's sacrament is lit up.
I muse on the loved mother and apostle at the cross, and Christ's Church is lit up.
I muse on the risen Christ at Lake Galilee, and all our Easters are lit up.
I muse on the eternal Lamb of God, and eternity's tenderness is lit up.

The King – Luke

The king creates order, balance, harmony. He is sure in his masculine identity. He is neither envious nor prejudiced. He integrates clashing forces. He stands firm, remains calm, provides shelter, fertilises seeds in people. He looks upon the world with a firm but kindly eye. He sees others in their weaknesses and talents; he accepts and encourages, honours and promotes them. He becomes a centre of stability and sustains centredness in others.

Luke was, of course, a doctor, but he has many kingly qualities. As we gaze at the portrait of Luke, we see a strong, calm person of authority whose eyes oversee everything. He is fleet of foot – his feet barely touch the footstool. Calves give their skin for the vellum on which Gospels are transcribed, but this calf, spread out right across the page, looks down with attentive eyes – nothing much is missed. The yellow of the cow's aura impacts the observer. This could be 'the cow that jumped over the moon'.

Luke has much more to observe, to think about, before he writes. He is observant, aware. He is the king. He gathers information and people. He writes the books. He befriends rulers and intimates of Jesus. He is an artist as well as a physician, companion and writer.

Luke's concerns encompass women and the marginalised, Greeks and not just Jews. He is at ease with the Greek as well as the Jewish worlds. He addresses his second volume (the Acts of the Apostles) to Theophilus, who may have been an actual or a symbolic Roman figure of authority. He gathers together information from sources that others had not connected. In his Gospel, women and other marginalised groups have an honoured place. In the Acts he describes how

Christianity was inculturated in Greek-speaking parts of the Roman Empire far beyond Judea.

> Stand astride.
> Become a still presence.
> Relax into your calling in God, like a tree secure in its roots.
> Make room for all but stand for something eternally significant.

Conclusion

I do mind–body exercises upon waking each day, and I recommend these. Start by stretching in a warrior-like crouch, arms stretched forward above the bent knee and say, 'I arise today in the strength of God the Warrior, the Creator, Initiator and Overcomer.' Let these words become your motivation. Secondly, touch your eyes and say, 'I arise today in the flow of the Shaper.' Make moving, supple body shapes that stretch, as a shaper, your seeing, sensing and connectivity. Thirdly, as you say, 'I arise in the name of the Lover, with all my senses', crouch down and allow God's divine sensing to spread through each part of your being. Pray, 'God bless each thing my hands touch, each thing I think, each word I speak, each soul I meet until I reach my home.' Fourthly, as you say 'I arise in the centredness of the King', stand with feet astride and hands stretched out. Encompass all, stand firm before any looming troubles, allow the quiet authority of the King of kings to reside in his royal child.

5. Resources and liturgies that celebrate the *Lindisfarne Gospels*, Northumbrian saints and our multicultural world

(a) *The Lindisfarne Gospels*

A *Lindisfarne Gospels* Benedicite

The Benedicite is the song of praise uttered by Shadrach, Meshach and Abednego when they remained unharmed after being cast into the fiery furnace by King Nebuchadnezzar for refusing to adore a golden statue he had set up. It is recorded in the apocryphal book of The Song of the Three Jews as an addition to the book of Daniel (additions to the book of Daniel 3:57-88, 56). Churches have widely used it for Morning Prayer and have sometimes adapted it, as I have below.

We bless you, glorious God of our forebears.
We bless you too for the fruit of their labours.
We bless you, God of Aidan and Cuthbert.
May holy lives bless you for ever.
We bless you for Eadfrith, Ethilwald and Billfrith.
May scribes and artists bless you for ever.
We bless you for calf skins and feather pens.
May all gifts of creation bless you for ever.
We bless you for colours and pigments and dyes.
May lapis lazuli and woad bless you for ever.
We bless you for the four Evangelists.
May truths of your word bless you for ever.
We bless you for your holy cross.
May cross-carpet pages bless you for ever.
We bless you for your creatures on earth.
May dogs and birds bless you for ever.

We bless you for your unending love.
May circles and twinings bless you for ever.
We bless you for the *Lindisfarne Gospels.*
May gleanings of heaven bless you for ever.
We bless you for this portal of prayer.
We praise and glorify you for ever.

A kontakion for the *Lindisfarne Gospels*

A kontakion is an unfolding hymn, a sermon in verse, which dates at least from sixth-century Byzantium. Its meaning derives from the Greek word for 'pole', specifically the pole around which a scroll is wound. It may be chanted or accompanied by quiet background music. The following kontakion does not follow the complete metrical form generally used in the East.

All glory to you, O God, for the Gospels of Lindisfarne,
a jewel shining in dark ages, that sheds light on your servants still.

All glory to you for the *Gospels,* transcribed by Bishop Eadfrith.
Blemishes were removed, beautiful letterings were made.
Billfrith the anchorite wondrously enriched it with gold
and Ethilwald had it bound in shining metal, enriched by the wondrous work of smiths.

All glory to you, O God, for the Gospels of Lindisfarne,
a jewel shining in dark ages, that sheds light on your servants still.

All glory to you for inspiration from Ireland, Egypt and Rome,
for Byzantines and Anglo-Saxons, and Britons nearer home.
All glory to you for the Muslims, the carpets and mats for prayer.
For knotwork, Evangelists, creatures, and for trumpets that fill the air.

All glory to you, O God, for the Gospels of Lindisfarne,
a jewel shining in dark ages, that sheds light on your servants still.

All glory to you for Cuthbert, Aidan and Oswald,
who fashioned a home worthy of the *Gospels*
and brought this first fruits of the Gospel to the English people.
All honour be to the communities of Lindisfarne and Durham and to the web of English worldwide.

All glory to you, O God, for the Gospels of Lindisfarne,
a jewel shining in dark ages, that sheds light on your servants still.

A liturgy of the *Lindisfarne Gospels*

Reading: John 20:30, 31
In Latin and/or in English:

> Now Jesus did many other miraculous signs in the presence of his disciples, which are not written in this book. But these are written so that you may come to believe that Jesus is the Messiah, the Son of God, and that through believing you may have life in his name.

This priceless jewel, the *Lindisfarne Gospels*, is dedicated to God. Let us give glory to God.

Hymn

Taize chant:
Glory to God, glory to God,
I will exult and sing to God my Saviour.
Glory to God, glory to God,
glory to you my God. Amen.

This jewel is also dedicated to Saint Cuthbert, shepherd and prophet, healer and evangelist, bishop and hermit soldier of Christ, the one who, when people confided in him their sins, and when he presided at the Eucharist of the Saving Victim, shed tears from his heart.

Sing

'Kyrie eleison'

Reading: Psalm 119:9-16

Sing

'Spirit of God, unseen as the wind'
Tune: 'Skye Boat Song'

Reading

This riddle from the tenth-century Exeter Book *describes the creation of an illuminated gospel from the preparation of vellum to the addition of gold ornamentation to the binding.*

An enemy ended my life, deprived me of my physical strength: then he dipped me in water and drew me out again, and put me in the sun, where I soon shed all my hair. After that, the knife's sharp edge bit into me and all my blemishes were scraped away; fingers folded me and the bird's feather often moved over my brown surface, sprinkling meaningful marks. It swallowed more wood dye and again travelled over me, leaving black tracks. Then a man bound me, he stretched skin over me and adorned me with gold; thus I am enriched by the wondrous work of smiths, wound about with shining metal.

The school, the scriptorium; the calves and the vellum; the pigments and the pens. Out of Eadfrith's pen came this glory of the north:

Divine Artist,
you endow us with gifts and call us to serve.
Anoint us by your Spirit that we, like your servant Eadfrith,

whose inspired fingers moved the bird's feather over the stretched, brown skin of calf, may make good use of our gifts and be worthy of our calling.

We give thanks for the gifts that came to us from Ireland.
We give thanks for the gifts that came to us from Rome.
We give thanks for the gifts that came to us from the East.
We give thanks for the gifts from England, our home.

Thank you for the multicoloured tapestry that makes up the indigenous English (or British) spirituality of whose birth is this book is a sign.
We give you thanks, O Lord.
For discipline and faithful workmanship,
We give you thanks, O Lord.
For delight and inspired workmanship,
We give you thanks, O Lord.

The three marks of English Spirituality

We invoke for churches of English-speaking people the three gifts highlighted in the text of the Gospels.

(1) The gift of Blessed Simplicity

> Let your word be 'Yes, Yes' or 'No, No'; anything more than this comes from the evil one.
> *Jesus, in the Sermon on the Mount (Matthew 5:37)*

We separate from all that is false in order to be united with all that is true:
simplicity in our speech, our activities and in the ordering of our lives;
purity in our motives;
transparency in our relationships.

Hymn

'Blest are the pure in heart'

(2) The gift of desert struggles over evil

Then the young warrior, God Almighty, stripped himself, firm and unflinching.
He climbed upon the cross, brave before many, to redeem humankind.
From 'The Dream of the Rood'

With Christ, to whom the spirits were subject,
we claim the victory of the Lord.
With the desert Christians, from whom the demons fled,
we claim the victory of the Lord.
With hermits who made wild places safe with prayer,
we claim the victory of the Lord.
With martyrs who vaulted over death,
we claim the victory of the Lord.
With Patrick who freed his land of serpent powers,
we claim the victory of the Lord.
With Aidan, who stilled the raging seas,
we claim the victory of the Lord.
With Oswald, who repelled the tyrant hordes,
we claim the victory of the Lord.
With Hilda, who released the song locked in a cowherd's heart,
we claim the victory of the Lord.
With Cuthbert, who stormed the gates of heaven,
we claim the victory of the Lord.
With the saints of this place,
we claim the victory of the Lord.
That the kingdoms of this world may become the kingdom of our God.

(3) Hospitality

Display a picture of Rembrandt's The Return of the Prodigal Son.

Reading: Luke 15:11-32

We are an inclusive church, but not one that stands for nothing. The Father retains his integrity – this enables him to reach out, unlike the self-righteous elder brother.

Prayer

Lord, the *Lindisfarne Gospels* reflect your many-splendoured heart of compassion towards all, and your desire to use the gifts of all, the gifts of creation – animal, vegetable and mineral – and the gifts of different races and cultures. Give us hearts that are wide open to your presence in all things and all people. Inspire us to encourage others to follow their calling. Weave us together in a multicoloured tapestry that illumines and inspires your world.

Hymn of celebration

For example, 'Come on and celebrate', 'Colours of day' or 'Now thank we all our God'.

There may be displays or projections of art and photography, flag or banner waving, music, dancing or singing by children or adults.

Hymn

1. Blessed home of glorious Gospels,
   nursery of saints and scribes.
   Fruit of years of faithful labour,
   surviving still both time and tides.
   Eadfrith scribing, Billfrith shrining
   Ethelwold – a glorious three.

2. Praise and honour to the Father,
praise and honour to the Son,
praise and honour to the Spirit,
ever Three, and ever One,
consubstantial, co-eternal,
while unending ages run.
Tune: 'Blessed City, Heavenly Salem'

Blessing

Let us go, inspired by this gracious gift,
to dedicate our talents to the glory of God,
to labour with painstaking love,
to do something beautiful for God.
And the blessing of God, Father, Son and Holy Spirit be with us for ever.

Prayers from Lindisfarne, home of the Gospels

To the prayers of the island saints we commend you.
May God's angels watch around you to protect you.
May the Holy Spirit guide and strengthen you for all that lies ahead.
May Christ Jesus befriend you with his compassion and peace.
Lord, be a bright flame before us.
Be a guiding star above us.
Be a smooth path beneath us.
Be a kindly shepherd behind us.
And the blessing . . .
The prayer offered to departing pilgrims by the parish church of Saint Mary the Virgin, Holy Island.

Circle me, Lord.
Keep peace within, keep evil without.
Keep protection near and danger far.
Circle me, Lord.
Keep light near and darkness far.[51]

(b) Eadfrith, Ethilwald and Billfrith

Eadfrith

Illuminator of the Lindisfarne Gospels, *bishop. Died 721. Feast day: 4 June.*

Introduction

In the mid tenth century, a monk named Aldred, in the Community of Saint Cuthbert at Durham, wrote this colophon, in early English, at the end of the Gospel of John:

> Eadfrith, bishop over the Church of Lindisfarne, first wrote this book in (honour of) God and St Cuthbert

Eadfrith was a monk of Lindisfarne who became its abbot and then its bishop. It was he who transcribed and illuminated the *Lindsfarne Gospels* in 698. His work reveals extraordinary scholarly and artistic qualities, and Eadfrith has been described as 'the first personality in English art history'. He died on 4 June 721 and his relics were taken with those of Aidan and Cuthbert, eventually to be buried in Durham.

In all monasteries of Columban foundation, the work of the scribe was held in great reverence and honour, after the example of Columba himself, who was an accomplished

51. This prayer of David Adam is printed on the reverse of the above pilgrims' prayer card.

penman and transcriber. It was a common practice to appoint a skilful penman as abbot or bishop, such as Dorbene of Iona and Eadfrith of Lindisfarne.

Prayer

Divine Artist,
you endow us with gifts and call us to serve.
Anoint us by your Spirit that we, like your servant Eadfrith, whose inspired fingers moved the bird's feather over the stretched, brown skin of calf, may make good use of our gifts and be worthy of our calling.

Readings

Psalm 45
Exodus 31:1-11
Luke 12:35-44

Ethilwald

Monk, Bishop of Lindisfarne, sponsor of the Lindisfarne Gospels *covers. Died 740.*
Feast day: 12 February.

Introduction

A disciple of Cuthbert, Ethilwald became Abbot of Melrose. He succeeded Bishop Eadfrith, scribe of the *Lindisfarne Gospels*, as Bishop of Lindisfarne, from 721 until he died in 740. He sponsored the hermit Billfrith to make the precious covers of the *Gospels*, which are now lost. His holy life was recognised by his relics being placed with those of Cuthbert and taken to Durham. He is the last Bishop of Lindisfarne to be revered as a saint.

Prayer

God of truth, God of beauty, who called Ethilwald to learn from your saints and to preserve the glories of your word, give us humility to learn its wisdom, that we may adorn your world with its eternal treasures.

Readings

Psalm 119:89-104
Deuteronomy 27:1-8
Matthew 13:45-52

Billfrith

Hermit and goldsmith.
Eighth-century feast day: 6 March.

Introduction

Billfrith was a hermit and goldsmith of Lindisfarne and a skilled worker in jewels and precious metals. When the pages of the *Lindisfarne Gospels* had been written and painted, they were bound in leather by Bishop Aethelweald, who then asked Billfrith to make a pattern of jewels embedded in the outer cover of the book. Billfrith adorned the cover with gold, silver and gems. Though the *Gospels* survive, the cover is now lost.

In the eleventh century, Billfrith's bones, which had been honoured, were taken by Alfred Westow, sacrist of Durham Cathedral. It is believed his relics were taken to Durham in the eleventh century, where he is celebrated with Baldred the hermit on 6 March.

Hermits such as Billfrith remind us of the great numbers of hermits in the history of the Church, and of their importance in keeping alive the ideals of austerity, devoted prayer and spiritual warfare.

Prayer

God our Eternal Treasure,
who gives glorious minerals to your creation and glorious skills to your people,
we bless you for the craft of Billfrith, honed in prayerful practice.
Raise up skilled craftspeople
who will use creation's gifts and their own for your glory.

Readings

Psalm 102:15-28
Exodus 37:1-16
Ephesians 6:5-8

(c) Cuthbert

Prayers and readings for a celebration of Saint Cuthbert.

Holy God of Cuthbert and the saints,
you bequeath to us rich treasures of grace.
God of the hills, God of the outposts,
you are present with us now.

Hymn

1. Saints of the Isles, rejoice,
   Brigid and Columcille,
   compassion's troubadours,
   you trod our fragile soil.

From Patrick's Mount to Brendan's Bay
you plumbed our depths and shared our toil.

2. Saints of the West, be glad;
David and Non uprise,
Illtyd and Samson too,
founders and teachers wise.
From Holywell to Bardsey Isle
their holy prayer to heaven cries.

3. Saints of the North, take heart;
Cuthbert and Mother Hild,
friends of the Servant Christ,
fierce warring souls you stilled.
From Eidyn's Rock to plague-struck homes
folks' minds you stirred, their hearts you filled.

Tune: 'Little Cornard'

Cuthbert received a call to ministry as he watched sheep on the Lammermuir Hills:

I lift up my eyes to the hills
where does my help come from?
My help comes from the Lord,
the Maker of heaven and earth.
He will not let you stumble –
he who watches over you will not sleep.
The protector of God's people never slumbers or sleeps.
The Lord will guard you;
he is by your side to protect you.
The sun will not hurt you by day,
nor the moon by night.

The Lord will protect us from all danger;
he will keep us safe.
He will protect us as we come and go, now and for ever.
From Psalm 121 (adapted)

Readings

Ezekiel 34:11-16
Micah 7:14a

My heart's desire

My heart's desire is to serve the King, to heed his call in everything.
My heart's desire is to touch his cloak, to release his power in ordinary folk.
My heart's desire is to storm heaven's gate till demons flee and storms abate.
My heart's desire is that sick are cured and that hostile mockers praise the Lord.
My heart's desire is that Christians are one in a Church in peace and communion.
My heart's desire is to reach the throne where God reigns in glory with his own.

Reading: John 10:11-18

Now, robed in stillness in this quiet place, emptied of all I was, I bring all that I am, your gift of shepherding to use and bless.[52]

Silence

52. Cuthbert's Prayer, Saint Aidan's Chapel, Bradford Cathedral.

Hymn

1. Saint of the Spirit's quest
and unremitting zest
for love divine;
carried in princely style
from your loved Holy Isle,
your body rests awhile
in Durham's shrine.

2. Monk of the open hand –
for Ripon's Melrose band
keeping the door;
off'ring a needed bed
to many a traveller's head,
sharing your wine and bread
with Christ's own poor.

3. Cuthbert, the otters' friend –
but first, to your life's end,
God's pray'rful priest.
From storm-swept island lair
teaching us all to share
the great Creator's care
for man and beast.

4. Help us, good northern Saint
to pray, and not to faint,
as once before
on Lindisfarne's rough land
with Aidan's crook in hand
you taught your pilgrim band
how to adore.

Edwin Le Grice © Copyright 2005 Kevin Mayhew Ltd
Tune: 'Moscow', The Celtic Hymn Book No. 164

Thanksgiving

Most glorious Giver of Life,
darkness and light praise you.
May stars and moon praise you.
The city and the country praise you.
May the rocks and the islands praise you.
The Gospels and the psalm books praise you.
May artists and poets praise you.
The guillemot and the gulls praise you.
May the ducks and the sea otters praise you.
Cuthbert and our risen ones praise you.
May all creation praise you and give you glory for ever.

Or

Thanks be to God for Cuthbert the boy,
who listened to an infant and heeded God's call.
Thanks be to God for Cuthbert the youth,
who prayed on a beach until God-mockers wondered.
Thanks be to God for Cuthbert the novice,
who studied well and grew strong in the Lord.
Thanks be to God for Cuthbert the healer,
who through prayer was healed and cured many sick.
Thanks be to God for Cuthbert the evangelist,
who rode to far parts and preached with power.
Thanks be to God for Cuthbert the prophet,
who warned brothers and royals of dangers ahead.
Thanks be to God for Cuthbert the soul friend,
who tenderly listened as folk laid bare their souls.
Thanks be to God for Cuthbert the prayer hermit,
who from Farne Isle stormed heaven's gates.
Thanks be to God for Cuthbert the man,
who in life and in death gave all for his God.

Intercessions

Lord, you called Cuthbert from the Border hills
to be a shepherd of the people
and a light to the land.
Call us to leave what lies behind us
and to reach out to others
until we, too, touch the gates of heaven.

Cuthbert's tender hands warmed cold feet and anointed sick bodies.
May your compassion flow through our hands.
May they offer a tender touch
and human warmth
to those who feel frozen out.

Kindly Cuthbert helped Lindisfarne's complaining monks,
unhappy under new regulations,
to make the transition from criticism to joy:
God of renewal, lead us
from complaining to appreciation,
from stagnation to creativity,
from coldness to love,
from ourselves to you.

None of those present would hide from Cuthbert the secrets of their hearts.
They cleansed themselves from the sins they had confessed by fruits of repentance.
May we foster the arts of the soul friend,
and walk in the light with one another.

Cuthbert went to poor and ignorant people
in remote and mountainous places which others dreaded to visit,
giving himself up gladly to this devoted labour.
Like Cuthbert, we would become
shepherds of your sheep,
peacemakers and hospitality givers,
open to change and partnership,
Spirit-led, in solitude and costly service.

Hymn

1. When the Church, in holy synod
   met by Alnmouth's sandy shore,
   with King Egfrith of Northumbria
   and Archbishop Theodore,
   to advance the Lord's own kingdom
   among those who had not heard
   the great message of salvation
   or the preaching of the word.

2. They elected as a bishop
   once a monk of Lindisfarne,
   holy Cuthbert, now a hermit
   on the isle of Inner Farne.
   Both the King and the Archbishop
   in a ship then set their sail,
   came as pilgrims to his island
   that their wishes might prevail.

3. Holy Cuthbert then surrendered
   to God's will, though grieving sore,
   and was consecrated bishop
   by Archbishop Theodore;
   first for Hexham, then returning

to Northumbria's Holy Isle;
very image of his Master
for a blessèd little while.

4. We have come, who here are gathered
to a great inheritance;
and the faith to us delivered
may we never leave to chance.
Strive we with our holy fathers
in their prayers and by their worth,
that the fullness of the kingdom
may be manifest on earth.
© Copyright Anthony Duncan
Tune: 'Daily, Daily', The Celtic Hymn Book No. 208

Shining stars

Cuthbert's call to serve God began as he sat under the night sky. His life also drew to a close under the night sky, for although his little hermitage on the Farne Isle had high, stone walls, its roof was open to the heavens.

Poem by Angus, aged six

My eyes like to see
the lovely stars in the sky
shining like diamonds and crystals,
and the sun above my head
and the moon shining and shining.

Eyes are shiny, too,
and the golden water shines.
My eyes like to see candles and the light in the sky.
God will give me a new heart
that shines with happiness inside me.

Closing blessing

May you keep God's peace and love among you.
Never look down on others.
Be of one mind.
Have goodwill towards those of different views.
Be hospitable and kindly towards all.
Based on Cuthbert's last words

(d) Aidan

Prayers and readings for a celebration of Saint Aidan

Today we thank God for Aidan, who knit together a commonwealth of races in the gospel and made Lindisfarne a cradle of the *Gospels.*

The following, or another hymn, may be sung

1. Ebb tide, full tide,
praise the Lord of land and sea;
barren rocks, darting birds,
praise God's holy name!

Refrain:
Glory to the High King, glory to his Son,
glory to his Spirit, ever three in one.

2. Poor folk, ruling folk,
praise the Lord of land and sea;
pilgrim sands, sea-shelled strands,
praise God's holy name!

3. Fierce lions, gentle lambs,
praise the Lord of land and sea;
noble women, mission priests,
praise God's holy name!

4. Chanting boys, slaves set free,
   praise the Lord of land and sea;
   old and young and all the land,
   praise God's holy name!
   © Copyright Ray Simpson
   The Celtic Hymn Book No. 43

As Aidan and the first 12 brothers, following a failed mission, journeyed with the gospel from western isle to eastern shore, what bridge did they fear to cross? What weakness filled them with doubt?

A candle or torch of flame is lit.

Reading

In Christ, our strength is made complete in weakness.
We carry a torch of living flame –
Christ, the Light of the world.

The light of Christ is among us:
in the gentle touch,
in the listening ear,
in the patient toil,
in the concern for the poor,
in the challenging of wrong.

When Aidan began his great mission, he put his trust in God and chanted many psalms.

Those who trust in God
are like a mountain that lasts for ever.
As the mountains surround Jerusalem,
so you surround your people.

The rule of wickedness shall not prevail
in the land you give to the godly.
Do good, O God, to those who are good,
to those whose hearts are true.
Echoes Psalm 125

We are told that Aidan was 'above anger and greed'. Let us confess the seeds of anger and greed that still lie within us.

Silence

Christ, have mercy.
Lord, have mercy.
Christ, have mercy.

Aidan went out with faith-sharing teams to tell the people the good news of Christ. He listened to the people, gave money to the poor, and bought slaves their freedom.

Old Testament readings: Isaiah 61:1-3 and/or Micah 6:8

May we speak truth to power, and may compassion move in places of influence.

Hymn

Here be the peace of those who do your sacred will;
here be the praise of God by night and day;
here be the place where strong ones serve the weakest,
here be a sight of Christ's most gentle way.
Here be the strength of prophets righting greed and wrong,
here be the green of land that's tilled with love;
here be the soil of holy lives maturing,
here be a people one with all the saints above.

Repeat

Ray Simpson, based on Aidan's 'Prayer for Holy Island'
Tune: 'Danny Boy', The Celtic Hymn Book No. 73

New Testament reading: Luke 6:17-20

Homily or address

Hymn

1. Saintly Aidan, priest of heaven,
saintly Aidan, priest of God:
selflessly his life was given
heralding the holy word.

2. At the Father's call compelling
to Iona's shores he came,
heart with Christian fervour swelling,
soul with Christian fire aflame.

3. Oswald for his aid beseeching,
Aidan to Northumbria trod,
swayed the heathen with his teaching
of the promised land of God.

4. Ever onward through the nation
faith-impelled he laboured on;
converts thronged in exultation
by his stirring message drawn.

5. Praise to Aidan, all-inspiring,
servant of the Father's will.
May we likewise toil untiring
Christian duty to fulfil.

Tune: 'Laus Deo', The Celtic Hymn Book No. 163

With loving kindness, Aidan brought the word of God – Christ's message of forgiveness and hope.
With gentleness, Aidan showed the people a new way through their fears and out of the darkness – a way of light and hope through Christ.
Help us to think your thoughts, to pray your prayers and to speak words that bring life to others.

Through dedication, self-discipline and study, Aidan showed his pupils a life of service and learning.
We will strive for learning in the service of Christ's Way.
Aidan made silent retreat that he might advance for God.
Restore our hearts to stillness; expand our hearts to love.

Hymn
'I, the Lord of sea and sky'
Daniel L. Schutte

Intercessions *One or more of the following may be used*
God of Aidan of simple dress,
give us the gift of simplicity.
God of Aidan of the gentle touch,
give us the gift of gentleness.
God of Aidan of the generous heart,
give us the gift of generosity.
God of Aidan of the ceaseless prayer,
give us the gift of prayer.
God of Aidan of the friendly greeting,
give us the gift of meeting.
God of Aidan of the burning faith,
give us the gift of believing.

Lord, you are my island;
in your bosom I nest.
You are the calm of the sea;
in that peace I rest.
You are the waves on the shore's glistening stones;
their sound is my hymn.
You are the song of the birds;
their tune I sing.
You are the sea breaking on rock;
I praise you with the swell.
You are the ocean that laps my being;
in you I dwell.
From *Liturgies from Lindisfarne*[53]

While Aidan was on retreat on Farne Isle, he saw an invading tyrant's forces set to destroy the king's headquarters by fire, and thus the Christian mission too. He raised his hands to heaven and said, 'Lord, see what evil he does.' The winds changed, the horses panicked, and the troops fled.
More things are wrought by prayer than this world dreams of. Let us intercede for victims of tyranny today.
See, Lord, what destruction is being wrought on your world.
Blow your winds, that the destroyers may change or retreat.
See, Lord, those abused at home, bullied at school, and exploited at work.
Blow your winds, that the destroyers may change or retreat.
See, Lord, the refugees, asylum seekers and victims of war.
Blow your winds, that the destroyers may change or retreat.

53. Simpson, Ray (Kevin Mayhew, 2010), prayer page 27.

A priest sent to escort the king's bride on an arduous sea voyage begged Aidan to pray for their safety. Aidan gave the escorts a flask of blessed oil. He prophesied: 'You *will* encounter storms, but remember to pour the oil on to the sea and it will become calm.'
All this happened as he had foretold. The waves swept over them and death seemed near, but when the priest poured the oil on the troubled waters, the sea became calm.

Divine Protector, pour your oil on the troubled waters of our lives.
We bring to you the troubles in our places of work . . .
God, we pray,
calm us, and help us rest in you.
We bring to you the troubles in our relationships . . .
God, we pray,
calm us, and help us rest in you.
We bring to you the troubles in our church . . .
God, we pray,
calm us, and help us rest in you.
We bring to you the troubles of the world . . .
God, we pray,
calm us, and help us rest in you.
Lord, you call us to pour oil on troubled waters.
Pour generously upon those we name before you now . . .
God, we pray, calm them,
and help them rest in you.

Hymn

'Eternal Father, strong to save'
(This has been described as the Holy Island anthem)

Blessing

Aidan served you with all his powers;
we will serve you with all our minds.
Aidan served others with all his love;
we will serve with all our hearts.
Aidan schooled his body and soul;
we will school our bodies and souls,
each day and night of our lives.

From today and always,
may we
look upon each person we meet
with the eyes of Christ,
speak to each person we meet
with the words of Christ,
and go wherever we are led
with the flame of Christ.

(e) Oswald

Introduction

Oswald's seventh-century reign was short but God-inspired, bold, energetic and civilising. Kingdoms speaking four different languages – British, Pictish, Irish and Anglo-Saxon – were linked together for the first time under his influence. He provided breathing space for perhaps the most significant mission to the English people ever to get under way, and permitted Aidan to establish a home for the *Lindisfarne Gospels*.

Hymn

1. Good King Oswald, glad returning
   from the fight at Heavenfield,
   called for Aidan wise, discerning,
   that his people might be healed,
   and, in holiness and learning,
   find, in Christ, their King, and yield.

2. King and Bishop rode together,
   preached the Gospel side by side;
   taught the Faith 'mid rocks and heather,
   forests, fields and stormy tide,
   fire and flood and wind and weather;
   standing always side by side.

3. Pray for us! You saints who founded
   this our Church in time long past.
   Pray for us! That we be grounded
   in true faith and hold it fast.
   Pray for us! That thus surrounded,
   we're found faithful at the last.

   © Copyright Anthony Duncan
   Tune: 'Traditional Welsh Melody', The Celtic Hymn Book No. 67

Reading: Psalm 72

Confession

There was once a popular saying: 'May God have mercy on their souls, as Oswald said when he fell to the earth.' Let us seek the mercy of God for all.
Bring us back, O God! Show us your mercy, and we will be saved.

Lord, have mercy.
Christ, have mercy.
Lord, have mercy.

Reading: Deuteronomy 17:14-19

We bring to you the lands of hate and conflict:
may these be seen as heaven's field.
We bring to you the lands of crop and dairy:
may these be seen as heaven's field.
We bring to you the lands of town and commerce:
may these be seen as heaven's field.
We bring to you the lands of home and leisure:
may these be seen as heaven's field.

Prayer

High King of heaven, who raised up Oswald to plant the healing tree of Christ's passion in his kingdom, redeem our land from the curse of disobedience and bring it under your just and gentle rule.

Reading: 1 Timothy 2:1-7

Hymn

1. Oswald on Iona, learning ways of God:
   Oswald on Iona, yoked to work and word.
   Oswald in Northumbria, spreading ways of God:
   Oswald in his kingdom winning subjects to his Lord.

   Refrain:
   Onward Christian pilgrims from training grounds of prayer, with shields of faith like Oswald's – new land cleansed and clear.

2. Onward Christian pilgrims, feuding slay and strife:
bring to lands long-blighted Christ's own love and life.
Onward Christian pilgrims, make Christ's folk a home:
let your words illumine them as through the land
they roam.

Refrain

3. Onward Christian pilgrims, have mercy on the poor:
give to Christ's proclaimers an ever-open door.
Onward Christian pilgrims, teach folk how to die:
confident in heaven, reborn eternally.

Refrain

Tune: 'St Gertrude'

Intercessions

Oswald was a man of prayer who rose early every morning to pray with the palms of his hands open to receive from God. We think Oswald was the first English ruler to appoint an officer to look after the needs of the poor.
We pray for the hungry, forgotten and lost.

Before Oswald fought the battle which won back his kingdom, he had a vision in the night in which Saint Columba assured him that God would be with him. Years after Oswald's death, a dying boy, along with some of the monks in a monastery at Bardney, had a vision in the night. Saint Oswald assured him that God would take him peacefully to the bliss of heaven, and that no more monks would die of plague.
O Christ, Son of the living God, may your saints and angels guard us in our sleep. May they reveal to us in our dreams visions of your glorious truth.

Oswald's personal influence continued after his death. The *Life* of Oswald caught the imagination of peoples of Europe who were looking for models of God-inspired leaders, and many churches in Europe are dedicated to him.
May the diverse authorities of our times acknowledge you as the Source of life, emulate you as the Servant King, and fear you as the Judge of truth.

Hymn

1. Aidan and Oswald, King,
   Finan and Colman too;
   Hilda, Enfleda, sing!
   Bede and Bartholomew.

   Refrain:
   At prayers of Northern Saints,
   we pray: save and defend us,
   Lord, this day.

2. Henry of Coquet, pray;
   Edbert and Robert, call;
   Cuthbert and Wilfrid, stay;
   hermits of Warkworth, all!

   Refrain

3. Oswin and Josephine,
   John and Paulinus true;
   you of the Church unseen,
   pray as we pray with you!

   Refrain

4. Peter and John and Paul,
who in his steps have trod;
Michael and angels all,
Mother of Christ our God.

At prayers of Northern Saints,
we pray: save and defend us,
Lord, this day.

Text © Copyright Anthony Duncan
Tune: 'Little Cornard', The Celtic Hymn Book No. 2

Closing prayers
The cross –
we shall take it.
The bread –
we shall break it.
The pain –
we shall bear it.
The joy –
we shall share it.
The gospel –
we shall live it.
The love –
we shall give it.
The light –
we shall cherish it.
The dark –
God shall perish it.
John Bell, Iona Community

May heaven's king go with you;
may Christ's cross grow in you;
may the Spirit's fire glow in you
till the final victory dawns.

(f) Hilda

Encouraged by Aidan of Lindisfarne, Hilda took monastic vows at the age of 33. After Aidan's death in 651, she became abbess of the largest faith community for both men and women among the English. She fostered vocations among many people, and hosted the 664 Synod of Whitby. She did much to make possible the fusion of different traditions in Northumbria's church which are reflected in the *Lindisfarne Gospels.*

Now let us praise the Birther of all,
the Guardian of the human race,
Holy Wisdom who binds the universe
in one free bond of love.

Hymn

The following (to the tune 'Ode to Joy' by Ludwig van Beethoven), or another hymn, may be sung.

Come you faithful through God's gateway,
to the door of Wisdom's home.
Enter in with hearts receptive,
making faith and truth your own.
Never doubting, never ceasing,
to your Saviour homage give.
Come you people, be upstanding,
ceaseless praises ever sing.

Psalm

Psalm 33:1-5, 20, 21
Psalm 34:1-10 or
Psalm 150

Hilda was constant in faith throughout her life;
forgive us for the times we have been faithless.
Hilda fostered excellence in all that was done;
forgive us for being content with the second rate.
Lord, have mercy.
Christ, have mercy.
Lord, have mercy.

Eternal God, who made the abbess Hild to shine like a jewel,
and through her holiness and leadership blessed your Church
with new life and unity,
help us, like her, to yearn for the Gospel of Christ
and to reconcile those who are divided.

Old Testament readings

Isaiah 61:10–62:5
Proverbs 8:1-16, 9:1-6 or
Wisdom 6:12-20

Hymn

1. A mother dreamed her child unborn
would shine like jewels, blazing bright.
From England's womb Hild leapt to life
and bathed the land in Christ's own light.

2. She fostered gifts in timid folk,
first English poet brought to flow'r
whose songs sped round the people's haunts
far from the corridors of power.

3. She mentored women called by God,
Elfleda, Heui,* and Bega too;
she taught her priests to live a life
which to their God the people drew.

4. Though sorely tried in mind and frame,
   she never ceased to give God praise;
   by night and day she said her prayers;
   Saint Hilda speaks to us always.

   * pronounced Hew

   Tune: 'O Waly Waly', The Celtic Hymn Book No. 8

Blessed are you, God of the planet Earth.
You have set our world
like a radiant jewel in the heavens
and filled it with activity, beauty, suffering
and hope.

Blessed are you, God of each land,
for giving Hilda as a radiant jewel
to light up the darkness of her people.
Faithful in both achievement and adversity,
constant in disappointment,
wise mentor, generous host,
counsellor of rulers, friend of cowherds,
encourager of talents,
able teacher, noble in bearing,
unceasing in praise.
Blessed are you, God of Hilda and her fellow saints.

New Testament readings

Matthew 13:31-33 or
Ephesians 4:1-13 or
Philippians 4:2-9

God of life,
help us to trade with the gifts you have given us.
Bend our minds to holy learning,
that we may escape the fretting moth of littleness
of mind that would wear out our souls.
Brace our wills to actions,
that they may not be the spoils of weak desires.
Train our hearts and lips
to songs which give courage to the soul.
Being reproved, may we give thanks,
and having failed, may we determine to succeed.
Echoes a homily of Hilda, anon

Hymn

1. Blessed Hilda, holy mother,
   friend of Aidan, Christ's own stalk;
   born to honour, stripped of father,
   finding faith, baptised at York;
   shining as a radiant jewel,
   lighting up our darkened walk.

2. Taught of God by Wearside river,
   daring, learning, steeped in prayer;
   you became a guide to many,
   friend of people far and near;
   drawing out the cowherd's talents,
   held by earth and heav'n most dear.

3. Faithful host and reconciler,
   staying true through shifting ties;
   thankful in success and trial,
   always fair and always wise;

meditator, motivator,
wisdom's gem, and heaven's prize.
© Copyright Ray Simpson
Tune: 'Westminster Abbey', The Celtic Hymn Book No. 22

Intercessions

Hilda discerned that God had given the gift of song to a shy, illiterate cowherd named Caedmon. Her students taught him Bible stories which became the first gospel pop songs in the English language.

A fragment of his song of creation speaks of the middle earth, which features strongly in J. R. R. Tolkien's *Lord of the Rings.* A school of poetry named after Caedmon flourished. Its flower is 'The Dream of the Rood' and the Ruthwell Cross. Our intercessions reflect these signs of God at work.

As Hilda drew out the songs the cowherd dared not sing,
bring to flower in your people the seeds that dormant lie.
We pray for those who have none to encourage them:
bring the seeds of confidence in them to flower.
We pray for those who are trapped by their circumstances:
bring the seeds of freedom in them to flower.
We pray for those who find it difficult to learn:
bring the seeds of understanding in them to flower.
We pray for those who feel powerless and without hope:
bring the seeds of empowerment in them to flower.
We pray for those who lack food or friendship:
bring the seeds of abundant life in them to flower.
We pray for those who are weak or nearing the end of their earthly journey:
bring the seeds of praise in them to flower.

Warm-winged Spirit, brooding over creation,
unlock the song in every human heart.
Draw forth the divine beauty
in every person on earth;
in women who feel degraded
and in men who abuse their role;
in children who are orphaned
and in the disabled who are frail.

After tending the community at Whitby for many years, that devoted servant of Christ, Hilda, suffered the trial of a long bodily illness, in order that, like the apostle Paul, her strength might be made perfect in weakness. A burning fever tortured her continually for six years, yet she never ceased to give public thanks to God night and day and to instruct her flock.

Worn by the cares of the day,
we offer you our praise.
Buffeted by trials,
we will not cease to return thanks to you.

Many beyond Northumbria's borders called Hilda 'Mother' because of her grace and wise counsel. In local legend, when the sea birds fly over Whitby Abbey, they dip their wings to acknowledge Hilda's presence that lingers still.

Hymn

'Embrace the universe with love, and shine with God in splendour'
© Copyright June Boyce-Tillman
Tune: 'St Columba', The Celtic Hymn Book No. 44

Closing prayer

Angels escorted Hilda to heaven.
We give thanks for your saints
who shine, like Hilda, in radiant brightness.
May the saints and the angels light up our path
and urge us on to heavenly virtues;
the virtues of peace and love,
devotion to you and justice to all,
wise friendship and a constant life,
faithful work and constant praise.

Attended by angels and the company of Hilda and of heaven,
we look to the Father and Mother of us all.
Earth mover, pain bearer, giver of life,
in joy we journey on.

(g) Wilfrid

Feast Day: 12 October

Wilfrid, the son of a Northumbrian thegn, was unhappy at home because of the unkindness of his stepmother. In his fourteenth year he was sent away to the Court of King Oswy, King of Northumbria. Here he attracted the attention of Queen Elfleda who sponsored him to study at Lindisfarne under Aidan, but he disliked the lack of grandeur in the Irish tradition. He journeyed to Canterbury and then to Rome, again sponsored by the queen, and was ordained.

Wilfrid was appointed Abbot of Ripon, displacing the guest master Cuthbert, who returned to Melrose, and was introduced to the Benedictine Rule there. At the Synod of Whitby in 664, his dominance was largely responsible for the victory of the Roman party over the Celts of Lindisfarne. When he was elected Bishop of York, he went to Compiegne to be consecrated by 12 Frankish bishops rather than risk any doubt of schism by being ordained by Celtic bishops. There were upsets, first with Chad and then with Archbishop Theodore of Canterbury, but the Roman authorities took his side and he was eventually restored to his see.

Wilfrid built magnificent stone churches at Ripon and Hexham and taught the Roman chant. He acquired vast landholdings and established monasteries in Northumbria, Mercia, Sussex and the Isle of Wight, and he converted Sussex, the last vestige of paganism, to Christianity.

He was the confidant of kings and queens but made many powerful enemies, and he was twice banished from Northumbria. He made three journeys on foot and horseback through Europe to Rome and was not afraid to seek papal jurisdiction over both crown and Church when he felt badly treated. His life was threatened many times: he was shipwrecked and nearly killed by natives off the coast of Sussex, imprisoned in Northumbria by the king and twice nearly murdered whilst travelling abroad.

After further disputes, Wilfrid resigned the see of York and became Bishop of Hexham, and spent his remaining years at Hexham. His gift to the English Church was to make it more clearly a part of the universal Church, but his manner and methods were not attractive.

The Roman strands in the *Lindisfarne Gospels* doubtless owe something to Wilfrid as well as to Benedict Biscop. Wilfrid's body was first buried in the crypt at Ripon but was subsequently transferred to Hexham.

Hexham Abbey uses the following prayer:

Almighty God,
who inspired Saint Wilfrid
to establish a religious community on this site
and to persevere after truth:
help us to know your presence among us now
and guide us as we seek to follow the way of Christ.

Readings

Psalm 103
Isaiah 52:7-10
Romans 10:11-15
Luke 5:1-11

Wilfrid's hagiographer, Eddius Stehanus, writes of his death at Oundle:

> The whole weeping community chanted prayers around his bed. As they reached Psalm 104 and the verse 'When you send forth your spirit they are created' (verse 30) his breathing ceased, and he yielded up his soul to his Creator. The aged soldier of God died more gently than an infant in the cradle.

Graham Usher, Director of Music at Hexham Abbey, wrote this lovely anthem of Saint Wilfrid in 2004:

VENI, Sancte Spiritus, reple tuorum corda fidelium,
et tui amoris in eis ignem accende.
V. Emitte Spiritum tuum et creabuntur;
R. Et renovabis faciem terrae.

COME, Holy Spirit, fill the hearts of Thy faithful
and kindle in them the fire of Thy love.
V. Send forth Thy Spirit and they shall be created;
R. And Thou shalt renew the face of the earth. Amen.

(h) Chad and the *St Chad Gospels*

Chad and his three English brothers were members of the first group of 12 boys chosen by Aidan when he started his first monastery school. Chad was a fine scholar who went to Ireland for further education. Chad's brother Cedd became Abbot of Lastingham, and upon his death from plague Chad took his place, and was later made Bishop of York. He graciously stepped down upon the arrival of Theodore as Archbishop of Canterbury, who doubted the validity of indigenous consecrations. Theodore was so struck by Chad's humility and spiritual stature that he asked him to become Bishop of the huge midland diocese of Mercia. Chad moved its centre from Repton to Lichfield, where he created prayer cells as a 'hearth' for the diocese. He travelled extensively and was much loved. He died of the plague, amid a vision of sweet angelic singing, in 672.

An illuminated book of Gospels was named after him (which also has various other names such as *The Lichfield Gospels* and *The Llandaff Gospels*). Michelle Brown describes it as 'the closest stylistic heir to the *Lindisfarne Gospels*'.[54] It is thought to be from the eighth century, and some scholars have suggested 730 as its date of origin.

The manuscript is also important because it includes, as marginalia, some of the earliest known examples of written Welsh. The first records in Latin the gift of the manuscript 'to God on the altar of St Teilo' by a man named Gelhi, who had bought the manuscript for the price of his best horse from Cingal. The 'altar of St Teilo' has in the past been associated with the monastery at Llandaff but, as it has been determined that the third, fourth and sixth marginal inscriptions refer to lands within 15 miles of Llandeilo Fawr,

54. Brown, *The Lindisfarne Gospels: Society, Spirituality and the Scribe*, p.381.

it is now thought that the book was given to the church there. It is now housed at Lichfield Cathedral. We may speculate as to whether the monks of Lichfield produced a *Gospels* in honour of Saint Chad within a generation of the *Lindisfarne Gospels* being dedicated to Saint Cuthbert.

A pilgrimage route has recently been named after Chad. St Chad's Way (named Saint Werberg's Way when travelling in the opposite direction) stretches 75 miles from the cathedral cities of Chester and Lichfield. It begins along the Shropshire Union Canal and proceeds to Nantwich via Beeston Castle, then eastwards across the M6 via Apedale to the Saxon Cross at Stoke Minster in Stoke-on-Trent. Thence it takes a southerly direction via the Trentham Estate, Stone and Stafford before ending at Lichfield. The Saint Chad project will link with the NHS, faith groups and other organisations that have a concern for healing and wholeness.

The idea for the footpath is the brainchild of experienced long-distance walker and Holy Island visitor David Pott. The former head teacher has also been deeply involved in various reconciliation initiatives including leading the Lifeline Expedition – a response to the legacies of the Atlantic slave trade – which has received widespread media attention. He says that early pilgrimage was especially associated with storytelling, such as the stories told in Chaucer's *Canterbury Tales*. Saint Chad's Way will include a story trail between Stoke and Stafford.

The Diocese of Lichfield has launched The Community of Saint Chad. This is for anyone in the Diocese 'who is prepared to journey with others in a quest for a life-changing faith'.[55] It invites people to commit to what it calls Five

55. The Community of Saint Chad. http://www.lichfield.anglican.org/assets/downloads/Community_of_Saint_Chad.pdf. Accessed 21 January 2013.

Rhythms, which include daily Bible reading, examination of conscience and undertaking a pilgrimage or retreat.

Faithful God, from the first fruits of the English people who turned to Christ, you called Chad to holy learning and high service as a missionary monk and bishop.
May we learn from his humility and loving discipline to pattern the ways of Christ in our time.

Chad would go into the church to pray when he heard wind or thunder. 'Don't you realise,' he explained, quoting Psalm 18, 'that God sends wind, lightning and thunder to excite earth's peoples to fear him, to humble their pride and make them aware that they will be judged?'

Reading: Psalm 18:1-19

Silence followed by the singing of 'Kyrie eleison'

Reading: 1 Samuel 3:1-10

Chad said he had never considered himself worthy of the post of bishop and readily resigned as Bishop of York, such was his humility.

The Song of Christ's Glory

Christ Jesus, though you were in the form of God, you did not cling to equality with God.
You emptied yourself, taking the form of a servant;
you were born in human likeness.
Being found in human form, you humbled yourself and became obedient, even to death on a cross.

Therefore God has highly exalted you
and given you a name above every other name.
That at the name of Jesus every knee should bow in heaven and on earth and under the earth.
And every tongue confess that Jesus Christ is Lord.
To the glory of God the Father. For ever and ever. Amen.
Philippians 2:6-11

It seems that Chad was the youngest, and the brightest, for he was sent to Ireland to do further studies. At this time, many young aspiring English Christians travelled round the cells of great Irish teachers. If necessary, the Irish gave them free board, tuition and even books, such was their generosity. It was said that Chad was 'learned in the Scriptures'.

Reading

2 Timothy 3:10-17 or
Luke 14:7-11

Hymn

'Spirit of God, unseen as the wind'
Margaret Old
Tune: 'Skye Boat Song'

Intercessions

God of the storm, God of the stillness,
of squalls of power and of shimmering calm,
into life's troughs and into life's billows
come with the reach of your long right arm.

Chad of the journey, Chad of the prayer,
of the humble heart and the teaching tales,
into life's troughs and into life's billows,
you bring God's presence that prevails.

King of kings, Source of all power, you remind us through your servant Chad that to clutch at position and power is of no use. As Chad willingly gave up status, yet eagerly developed his aptitudes to the full, so may we study and grow into the fullness of the calling you have for us, and be content with its dignity, gladly eschewing that which is not for us.

As we recall the rhythm of work and prayer at the community at Lastingham, the noise of hammer and chisel, the chanting of psalms, the study and the cooking, we pray that you will be with us in our work:
God of Chad and the willing heart, we come to you ready to do your will.

We pray for our schools and places of learning.
We pray for the cathedral and diocese of Lichfield,
and for the church at Lastingham.

Chad was mindful of his last end in all he did. Help us to keep always before us, O God, the fleeting nature of this life, and the eternal community for which we are destined. Knowing this, assist us
to banish ill will and the misuse of time and talents,
and help us to run the race you have chosen for us
with our eyes fixed on Jesus from beginning to end.

One day a brother heard sweet singing come from the highest point of the winter sun through the roof of the cell where Chad was praying, until it filled it. After half an hour, he heard the same joyful sounds return with unspeakable sweetness into the sky. As he was wondering what this could mean, the Bishop came to the window and clapped his hands, as was his custom when he wanted people to come to him. He told Owine to bring all the seven brothers, whom he urged to live in love and peace and to follow the Rule taught by Aidan with unwearying constancy, and to follow the example the spiritual fathers before him had set. Then he told them that 'the amiable guest', meaning the plague, would come for him in seven days. 'Commend me to God and prepare yourselves also to be ready to meet your God at any time,' he told them. Seven days later he did indeed die, and one of the brothers saw Chad's deceased elder brother Cedd coming with angels from heaven to greet him.

Hymn

'Angels singing'

Blessing

Grant us to drink in with joy
the word that gives knowledge of you,
that we may come at length to
stand before your face for ever.

(i) An Escomb Lament

The renewed focus on the *Lindisfarne Gospels* coincides with a renewed thirst for the Celtic strand that was woven into the *Gospels* but which became suffocated as the Church became top heavy.

The parish church at Escomb, by the river Wear, was established after Aidan's death but before the *Gospels* were produced. It is one of only three Anglo-Saxon church buildings from that time that is still regularly used for worship. The building contains Roman stone, and architecture showing both Irish and European influences. In recent years it has hosted multifaith gatherings under the umbrella name of *Celtic Springs*. There are no rules and there is no hierarchy, except that two 'gatekeepers' ensure that everything is said in love.

In 2012, a new development, termed 'Celtic Church', was launched. Normal Church of England services are maintained at the regular times, but on the afternoon of each fourth Sunday of the month a different congregation, the Celtic Church, meets. The theme of the first service was 'What springs of life are blocked that need restoring in order to heal people and the land?' Each person was invited to touch the mysterious 'fruit' carved on the ancient Celtic altar cross, and on their way back to bless themselves from a bowl of ancient local spring water. Afterwards, everyone took a stone that had been carried from the ford across the river that helped to make Escomb a spiritual centre and placed them outside in the shape of a Celtic cross.

The following prayers and Lament for the Synod of Whitby echo those used at Escomb. Although some sentiments expressed are rightly the subject of debate, there is no doubt that they reflect the views of many dechurched and unchurched people:

Mother and Father God, use us to restore true community of women and men, sharing hearts and materials.
Father and Mother God, use us to restore true care of the land, in simple living.

Mother and Father God, use us to restore true honouring of the beauty of the changing seasons and the myriad creatures.
Father and Mother God, use us to restore true honouring of the springs of the Spirit.
Mother and Father God, use us to restore true love between people and creatures, a love that cradles the best life for all.

The leaders in the Church gathered at Whitby in 664.
Arise, O Celtic holy women.
Celtic voices spoke for the mountains and the islands and the people.
Arise, O Celtic holy men.
But the power of the continental Church turned the others.
Arise, O Celtic holy women.
And so the Synod pledged the land to the Holy Roman Empire.
Arise, O Celtic holy men.
The Celtic ways were soon called wrong and primitive and dark.
Arise, O Celtic holy women.
All the Celtic beauty was pushed to the margins.
Arise, O Celtic holy men.
But the springs of the Spirit of the land remained under the ground.
Arise, O Celtic holy women.
In our days the Empire is dying and the Celtic springs flow stronger.
Arise, O Celtic holy men.
May we take up the vision of the Celtic founders of this holy place.
Arise, O Celtic holy women.
May we join in the flow of these ancient ones.
Arise, O Celtic holy men.

May the healing rivers of the gentle Spirit return to our barren land.
Arise, O Celtic holy women and men.

(j) Prayers for the Hours – Coptic, Celtic, 24–7

The Coptic Church has sustained the seven canonical 'hours' of prayer of the universal Church to this day. The core is the chanting or recitation of the psalms.

Generally in a country like Britain, although Muslims pray five times a day, Christians do so only if they are in a monastery. Now, however, movements of lay Christians inspired by the heritage that is reflected in the *Lindisfarne Gospels*, such as my own Community of Aidan and Hilda, are committing to daily prayer stops that reflect the rhythm of the sun. The number of these prayer stops typically varies from between two and five. The 24–7 prayer movement has introduced the practice of prayer around the clock for a 24-hour period, usually by rota.

Here are some tasters drawn from Coptic and Aidan and Hilda usage. The words in brackets are the Latin terms some churches use.

First hour (Prime) – about 6 am

Jesus prayed early in the morning, and this hour commemorates the resurrection of the Lord (Psalm 62:1). Try a 'rising-up prayer' such as the following:

I arise today in the strength of the Father.
I arise today in the radiance of the Son.
I arise today in the renewing of the Spirit.
I arise today in the Three-in-One.

Third hour (Terce) – about 9 am

In this hour of the day, the Holy Spirit came down upon the Apostles as tongues of fire (Acts 2:1-15). At this hour also, our Lord Jesus Christ was condemned.

Shine on us, Lord, like the sun that lights up day.
As day follows night, bathe us in your glory.

Sixth hour (Sext) – about midday

At this hour, our Lord Jesus Christ was crucified (John 19:14-16).

As the press of work pauses at noon, may your Spirit rest upon us.
As the sun rides high at noon, may the Sun of Righteousness shine upon us.
As the rain refreshes the stained, stale street, may your Spirit bring rain upon our dry ground.

Ninth hour (None) – about 3 pm

Remember that at this hour Jesus died on the cross.
Remember also the testimony of the thief at his right hand (Luke 23:40-42).

As you died at this hour for me,
help me to put to death my destructive cravings and to remain true to you.
I pray also for the people of the world
who suffer the heat and burden of the day.
Give them your peace.

Twelfth or eleventh hour (Vespers) – about 6 pm

Instituted to commemorate the removal of the body of the Lord Jesus Christ from the cross, the wrapping of it in linen and the anointing of it with sweet spices. Churches and households have an Evening Prayer service about this time.

Fifteenth hour (Compline or Night Prayer) – about 9 pm or before bed

This hour commemorates the laying down of the body of Christ in the grave. It corresponds to the last hour of the day before retiring, since sleep is but a temporary death (Psalm 62:6).

May angels guard us while we sleep.
Awake, may we watch with Christ; asleep, may we rest in peace.

Eighteenth hour (Midnight)

A few who do this in monasteries, or during a dedicated vigil, or because they do shift work, or because they cannot sleep, recall the three times our Lord prayed in Gethsemane (Matthew 26:36-46). Remember also that the Jewish people were led out of slavery in Egypt at midnight (Exodus 12:29-34). Jesus is expected to come again as a thief in the night (1 Thessalonians 5:2).

Shepherd of souls, I remember before you all those who have died in you and live with you.
Shepherd of souls, you watch over those who cannot sleep. I use this time to pray for those for whom I have a concern . . .

Twenty-first hour – about 3 am

This reminds us that Jesus was raised early in the morning, 'while it was still dark' (John 20:1).

Risen Christ, be my light in the darkness. Shine on all who plan dark deeds and relight their path.
Shine on all who sleep but know you not . . .

In the Coptic tradition . . .

. . . at the start of each of the hours the worshipper prays:
In the name of the Father, and the Son, and the Holy Spirit, one God. Amen.
Kyrie eleison, Lord have mercy, Lord have mercy, Lord bless us. Amen.
Glory be to the Father, and to the Son, and to the Holy Spirit, both now and ever and unto the ages of ages. Amen.

The Lord's Prayer

Prayer of thanksgiving

Let us give thanks to the beneficent and merciful God, the Father of our Lord, God and Saviour, Jesus Christ. For he has shielded us, rescued us, kept us, accepted us unto him, had compassion on us, supported us, and brought us unto this hour. Let us ask him also to keep us this holy day and all the days of our life in all peace, the Almighty Lord our God.

O Master, Lord, God Almighty, Father of our Lord, God and Saviour Jesus Christ, we thank thee upon every condition, for any condition, and in whatever condition. For thou hast shielded us, rescued us, kept us, accepted us unto thee, had compassion on us, supported us and brought us unto this hour. Therefore we ask and entreat thy goodness,

O Lover of man, grant us to complete this holy day, and all the days of our life, in all peace with thy fear. All envy, all temptation, all the influence of Satan, the intrigue of wicked people, the rising up of enemies, hidden and manifest, take away from us, and from all thy people and from this, thy holy place.

But as for those things which are good and useful, provide us with them. For thou art the One who gave us the authority to trample on serpents and scorpions and every power of the enemy.

And lead us not into temptation, but deliver us from the evil one, through the grace, compassion and love of man, of thine only begotten Son, our Lord, God and Saviour, Jesus Christ. Through whom glory, honour, dominion and worship befit thee with him and the Holy Spirit, the life-giver who is of one essence with thee, both now and ever, and unto the ages of ages. Amen.

Psalm 50

(k) A liturgy of the Desert Athletes of Christ

Jesus said, 'Go into your room and shut the door and pray to your Father who is in secret' (Matthew 6:6).

The Desert Fathers and Mothers said, 'Go to your cell and your cell will teach you all things.'

God, make my heart a little home,
everything in which you own.
God, make my heart a little cell,
where hell's detritus I dispel.

God, make my heart a little gym,
where everything is kept in trim.
God, make my heart an altar pure,
where you are placed for evermore.

Therefore, since we are surrounded by so great a cloud of witnesses, let us also lay aside every weight and the sin that clings so closely, and let us run with perseverance the race that is set before us.
Hebrews 12:1

By abstaining from things that harm body or soul,
we will run with the Athletes of Christ.
By resisting the temptations of the evil one,
we will run with the Athletes of Christ.
By dethroning the eight deadly sins,
we will run with the Athletes of Christ.
By striving that nothing is in us but love,
we will run with the Athletes of Christ.

(l) Multicultural prayers

The family of monasteries founded by Saint Columba was involved in the seventh-century controversy about the date of Easter. It is perfectly possible that Aidan attended one of the Irish monasteries such as Durrow, where Cummian, as some think, was Abbot, or was certainly a leading voice in that area. Cummian received a letter from the Pope, studied the Easter question exhaustively, and at first encouraged his Irish compatriots to change over to the Roman date. However, Segene, Abbot of the Iona mother monastery of the Columban family of Irish monasteries, strongly disagreed.

Aidan himself accepted the approach that the Columban monasteries had agreed. We do not know what he privately thought was the best approach. We do know, however, that some of his spiritual children migrated to Ireland rather than accept the new regulations, and that others of his spiritual children, who did not have that option, worked to build good relationships under the new framework.

Michelle Brown thinks that, on balance, Lindisfarne was the most likely venue for the fusion of influences that made up the *Gospels*. She writes of 'a fully integrated, synthesised Insular culture which was confidently sited within the broader Christian ecumen'.[56]

Some diversity-weaving prayers

Divine weaver,
shift us from a black and white view of the world, where people can only be friends and foes, and help us to weave a multicoloured tapestry of God's entire human family.

We bless you for the many-coloured tapestry which is your Church.
We grieve with you that so many strands have been torn apart.
Weave together in us,
scriptural holiness and a catholic spirit,
pentecostal callings and contemplative calm,
radical justice and sacramental grace,
that we may reflect your body on earth
as it is in heaven.

56. Brown, M. *The Lindisfarne Gospels: Society, Spirituality and the Scribe*, p.397.

In each hidden thought our minds start to weave,
be our canvas and our weaver.
Weave meaning out of memory,
that we may gain insight from inspired people
and grow into the wholeness of Christ.

We weave this day
silence of knowing,
clearness of seeing,
grace of speaking.
We weave this day
humility of listening,
depth of understanding,
joy of serving.
We weave this day
peace of being,
gift of loving,
power of meeting.

We leave this place
strengthened to share Christ's gospel,
loved to serve Christ's weak ones,
freed to weave Christ's patterns.

A Northumbria Benedicite

Bless the Holy One, all created things;
to whom be glory and praise for ever!
Bless the Holy One, you uncreated beings;
to whom be glory and praise for ever!
Bless the Holy One, sun and moon.
Bless the Holy One, clouds and sky.
Bless the Holy One, rain and wind;
to whom be glory and praise for ever!

Bless the Holy One, cold and heat.
Bless the Holy One, winter and summer.
Bless the Holy One, earth and sea;
to whom be glory and praise for ever!
Bless the Holy One, all that grows in the ground,
barley and beet, berry and bean.
Bless the Holy One, all that swims in the waters,
salmon and seal, oyster and eel.
Bless the Holy One, all that flies in the air,
gannet and gull, tern and cuddy duck.
Bless the Holy One, all people on earth;
to whom be glory and praise for ever!

A multicultural Benedicite

We who are created bless you.
Abraham, the father of Christians, Jews and Muslims blessed you.
We, too, of many faiths, bless you.
Moses and Miriam blessed you.
We, too, male and female, bless you.
David praised you, the king of the great heart.
May music and dance praise you.
The Scribes praised you.
May gold and pigments, cloth and caskets praise you.
You have made of one blood all the peoples on the earth.
Black and white, brown and yellow – we, too, praise you.
The creator of earth's four quarters blesses us.
North and south, east and west praise you.
The Mind from whom all thought comes blesses us.
Thinking and writing bless you.
The artist from whom all sights come blesses us.
May painting and poetry praise you.

The seven days and the seasons praise you.
And we, too, shall praise you, eternal King of glory.
Echoes a Celtic British act of praise from Taliesin

We bless the Source of the unfolding cosmos who breathes life into all.
We bless the Source of all,
who gives thoughts to minds and moves bodies to dance with delight.
We bless the Source of all,
who works in us with sighs, hopes and symbols too deep for words.
We bless the Source of all,
who in our pain energises us and calls us to live in solidarity with the vulnerable.
We bless the Source of all,
who unmasks lying words and deceitful hearts.
We bless the Source of all,
who delights in diversity and calls us to respect differences.
We bless the Source of all,
who tenderly fosters people of every temperament, ability and colour.
We bless the Source of all,
who delights in patterns, colours and words that make the Gospel glorious.
We bless the Source of all.

6. More hymns of Northumbrian saints

1. All glory to God who, in mercy and grace,
has fostered a home in this pilgrimage place.

Praise God! Praise God! Praise you for your saints!
Praise God! Praise God! Praise you for your saints!

2. From Ireland Columba sailed over the sea
and built on Iona a large monast'ry.

3. Northumbria's Oswald to Christ there did yield
then turned his new kingdom into heaven's field.

4. For Aidan the gentle brought faith to a land:
and many rough English joined Christ's faithful band.

5. A line of great Christians like Cuthbert appeared
who healed many people whom once they had feared.

6. Like Hilda, the teacher of wisdom to all,
who mentored the many and shone like a jewel.

7. When tyrants in Europe had turned a dark page
these saints changed it into a new Golden Age.

8. They gave us the *Gospels* and jewels of grace
and beckon us now to run our great race.

Tune: 'Lourdes', The Celtic Hymn Book No. 6

Hymn of the Church of Northumbria

1. God of all the ages
hallowed be thy name;
saintly lives are pages
in thy book of fame;
poets, priests and preachers,
scribes with patient pen,
humble-hearted teachers
of their fellow men.
In their generation
making straight the road;
builders of a nation,
workers with our God.

2. North to Cumbrian regions
furthest fort of all,
rode the Roman legions
watchmen of the wall;
where the fierce marauder
planned his dark foray,
Roman peace and order
brought a brighter day.
For to that lone station
Christian soldiers came
bearing Christ's salvation,
bowing at his name.

3. From the Roman city
was Augustine sent,
messenger of pity
to the men of Kent,
nor were heralds silent

in the distant north,
from Iona's island
to the Firth of Forth.
  Mark we well the story
  how the word was sent,
  giving God the glory
  in each sacrament.

4. King beyond the Humber
Edwin sought and found
one to wake from slumber
pagan lands around;
to his high task rising
toiled Paulinus on,
preaching and baptising
high at Holystone.
  Heathen hosts invaded;
  frail Paulinus fled;
  Thanes were slain, homes raided;
  could the Faith be dead?

5. Lord, thy torch is burning
by the western sea;
Celtic priests are yearning
realms to win for thee;
apostolic number
sails from Erin's land,
led by loved Columba
to Iona's strand.
  Fishers from the Islands,
  shepherds in Strathclyde,
  clansmen of the Highlands
  own the Crucified.

6. Oswald, the true-hearted,
once he saw the light,
for the faith imparted
fought a hero's fight;
when Cadwalla's masses
strove to cross the Tyne,
ere the pagan passes
sets the Cross his sign.
Stands his ground undaunted
till the foe must yield;
where the cross he planted
called they Heavenfield.

7. From Iona, Aidan
came to Oswald's home,
to the heavy laden
spake of rest to come,
led by love unbounded,
in his Master's name.
With his monks he founded
Holy Island's fame.
Lowly huts their dwelling
under Celtic rule,
love of God forthtelling
in a prophet's school.

Tune: 'St Gertrude'

1. Glory to the Father,
glory to the Son,
glory to the Spirit;
ever Three-in-One.

2. Praise for those who mirrored
triune Love on earth;
shining in Bede's pages
signs that life has worth.

3. Thank you for Bede's learning,
for his ready pen,
for a lifetime's labours
crowned with heav'n's 'Amen!'

4. Kneeling at his dying,
brothers at his side;
chanting to his maker
at Ascensiontide.

5. Glory to the Father,
glory to the Son,
glory to the Spirit;
ever Three-in-One.

Tune: 'Caswall', The Celtic Hymn Book No. 58

1. Proud, yet humble, strong and gentle,
from Iona's holy shore,
Aidan to King Oswald's princedom
Christian joy and radiance bore.

2. Where the ruthless zeal of others
quenched the smould'ring flax of love,
Aidan warmed the coldest spirits
with the fire from heav'n above.

3. At the quest of kings and rulers
seated at the royal right hand,
Aidan shared both food and silver
with the poorest of the land.

4. Staff in hand, Christ's shepherd journeyed
over northern dale and moor
bringing vision, faith and friendship
to the outcast and the poor.

5. Lindisfarne, his Holy Island,
wild, yet tranquil, windswept, fair,
nurtured in severe seclusion
northern saints and folk of prayer.

6. Cuthbert, Cedd and Chad and Hilda,
folk of courage, faith and fire,
bright with Aidan's Celtic vision
still today our lives inspire.

7. In the joy of God the Spirit
to the Lord of all we bring
praise for folk of northern England,
servant saints of Christ the King.
Edwin Le Grice © Kevin Mayhew Ltd
Tune: 'Shipston', The Celtic Hymn Book No. 160

Bibliography

Books

Adam, David, *Cry of the Deer* (SPCK Classics, 2009)

Backhouse, Janet, *The Lindisfarne Gospels: Society, Spirituality and the Scribe* (Oxford 1981, reprinted 1992)

Bede, *The Ecclesiastical History of the English People* (Penguin, 2003)

Bonner et al, *St Cuthbert, His Cult and His Community to AD 1200* (Boydell, 1989)

Brown, Michelle P., *Painted Labyrinth: The World of the Lindisfarne Gospels* (British Library, 2004)

Brown, Michelle P., *The Book and the Transformation of Britain c. 550-1050: a Study in Written and Visual Literacy and Orality* (British Library, 2012)

Brown, Michelle P., *The Lindisfarne Gospels: Society, Spirituality and the Scribe* (University of Toronto Press)

Brown, Michelle P., *The World of the Lindisfarne Gospels* (British Library, 2004)

Calkins, Robert G., *Illuminated Books of the Middle Ages* (New York: Cornell University Press, 1983)

Clayton, Ewan & Cooper, Robert, *Embracing Change: Spirituality and the Lindisfarne Gospels* (Clare Clayton, 2003)

Coatsworth, E. & Pinder, M., *The Art of the Anglo-Saxon Goldsmith, Fine Metalwork in England, its Practice and Practitioners* (Woodbridge, 2002)

Crossley-Holland, Kevin (trans), *The Anglo-Saxon World* (Boydell & Brewer, 1994)

Dales, Douglas, *Called to be Angels* (Canterbury Press, 1998)

Giles, J. A. (trans), *Ecclesiastical History of the English Nation* (London: J. M. Dent; New York: E. P. Dutton, 1910)

Jerome, *Commentary on Ezekiel 1:7* (Cambridge University Press, 1980)

Millar, Eric George F. S. A., *The Lindisfarne Gospels* (British Museum, 1923)

Mitton, Michael, *Restoring the Woven Cord: Strands of Celtic Christianity for the Church Today* (BRF, 2009)

Plummer, Charles (ed), *Irish Litanies: Text and Translation* (Henry Bradshaw Society) Vol. LXII

Schaff, P. (ed), *Jerome: The Principal Works of St Jerome* (http://www.ccel.org/ccel/schaff/npnf206.iv.II.html)

Simpson, Ray, *High Street Monasteries: Fresh expressions of committed Christianity* (Kevin Mayhew, 2009)

Simpson, Ray, *Liturgies from Lindisfarne* (Kevin Mayhew, 2010)

Taylor, Thomas (trans), *The Life of Samson of Dol* (Llanerch Press)

Webb, J. F. (trans), *The Age of Bede* (Penguin, 1998)

Winterbottom, Michael, *Gildas: The Ruin of Britain, and other works* (Phillimore, 1978)

Journals and magazines

The New York Review of Books

Websites

http://www.bl.uk/onlinegallery/ttp/lindisfarne/accessible/introduction.html

http://www.paracletepress.com/didache.html

http://www.aidanandhilda.org

Liturgical resources from Ray Simpson

The following titles are all available from Kevin Mayhew:

The Celtic Prayer Book in four volumes:

1. Prayer Rhythms	1500591
2. Saints of the Isles	1500592
3. Healing the Land	1500607
4. Great Celtic Christians	1500697
The Celtic Hymn Book	1413262
Liturgies from Lindisfarne	1501225

For details of all Ray Simpson's titles visit
www.kevinmayhew.com

Matthew

Mark

Luke

John